Forge Ahead

The Blueprint to Creating a Winning Strategy in Business, Life, and Wrestling

BY

Frank Vitale

Copyright © 2024 by Frank Vitale

All rights reserved. No part of this publication may be reproduced, distributed, or transmitted in any form or by any means, including photocopying, recording, or other electronic or mechanical methods, without the prior written permission of the author, except in the case of brief quotations embodied in critical reviews and certain other non-commercial uses permitted by copyright law.

Ordering Information: Quantity sales. Special discounts are available on quantity purchases by corporations, associations, and others. Orders by U.S. trade bookstores and wholesalers.

DREAMSTARTERS

www.DreamStartersPublishing.com

Table of Contents

Dedication 4

Foreword 5

Testimonials 7

Introduction 9

Showing Up 13

Going Above and Beyond 20

Contributing At Your Best Level 27

Waste Nothing 45

Don't Be a Victim 56

Learning to Train, Visualize, and Execute 66

Service 75

The Power of Connectivity 82

Know Your Value 88

Stakeholder Importance 100

Engage the Critic 107

Blueprint Your Way 116

Process Is Critical 126

Give It Away 136

Conclusion 144

Acknowledgements 148

Dedication

For Ashley, Max, Izzy and Cece…Love

Foreword
By Tim Flynn

One of my guiding principles in life is "You Get What You Earn." It's not about getting what you want or dream of; it's about putting in the necessary work. To achieve your dreams and secure victories, one must be committed and disciplined. Success is earned, not deserved.

This mindset is crucial for success in life, business, and particularly in wrestling, and it is a mindset that Frank Vitale embodies as well.

I first met Frank shortly after I became the head wrestling coach at West Virginia University in 2017. Frank, a former wrestler, high school wrestling coach, and father of a high school wrestler, brought invaluable expertise to our regional training center. A few years ago, when we needed support with fundraising and related programming, Frank leveraged his strategic planning and business development skills to help us. He played a key role in developing and refining our goals for fundraising and establishing a long-term growth strategy. Frank introduced a business perspective to our collegiate athletic environment, helping us identify opportunities and share a vision for success.

Wrestling parallels business in many ways. Competitors may have advantages, customer demands may be challenging, and financial obligations may be burdensome. However, with determination, a solid strategy, discipline, and a focus on the end goal, success is attainable. Knowing your destination, planning the journey, and having a strong team to maintain focus, motivation, and accountability are essential.

Wrestling demands discipline, proper training, strength and conditioning, a balanced diet, rest, and a winning mindset. Technique is vital, and hard work is non-negotiable. Failure is part of the journey, but resilience is key. Wrestling teaches valuable life and business lessons.

Wrestling and business can both be humbling. During times of feeling overwhelmed or beaten down, having a clear vision and a success blueprint is crucial. "Forge Ahead – The Blueprint to Creating a Winning Strategy in Business, Life, and Wrestling" will transform your approach to strategy, tactics, and execution, both on and off the mat.

Tim Flynn, the ninth head wrestling coach in West Virginia University's history, earned All-American honors as a wrestler at Penn State University. Recognized as a NCAA Division I "Coach of the Year," Flynn is among the winningest active coaches in college wrestling.

Testimonials

"Frank is an outstanding leader with integrity and wonderful ideals."
— **Virgil I. Hill Jr., Rear Admiral U.S.N. (Retired), 53rd Superintendent of the U.S. Naval Academy and President of Valley Forge Military Academy & College**

"Frank Vitale portrays a relentless focus on growth and achievement. Every day he exhibits a sense of urgency and excitement; demonstrates candor, insight, and creativity; and thrives in an environment of change, challenge and competition. Those who have retained him often identify Frank as an effective demolition-man of bureaucracy and ambiguity. In my world he has become 'The Man to See' because he executes …. every time."
— **John Fahey, United Bank**

"Frank Vitale's strategic expertise is not just about making decisions but sculpting a legacy of innovation and growth. As a mentor and friend, he has also profoundly influenced my journey as a CEO. His insights have helped me redefine the essence of true leadership, teaching me that it's not the title that makes a leader, but the ability to inspire, empower, and elevate those around you to achieve greatness."

— Brandon Downey, Chairman and CEO Trilogy Innovations

"Frank's leadership has helped us grow our organization significantly every year. He's a focused strategist and has helped us navigate considerable challenges to overcome the severe knowledge gap in the veteran's business community concerning private sector contracting. His guidance has advanced our work, and his contribution has directly led to the U.S. military veteran community attaining greater post-military prosperity through entrepreneurship."

— Matthew Pavelek, President and CEO of NaVOBA (National Veteran-Owned Business Association)

Introduction

Making smart, strategic choices in your business means finding the right resources, aligning your goals, and empowering your own potential.

Succeeding in business, and in every aspect of your life, is all about going forward. Even if you're on the bottom right now, you can score the success you desire and achieve your business goals.

Creating Forward Momentum

Connecting possibilities, sharing critical lessons, and utilizing technical applications all create forward movement, igniting the possibilities in your life.

You must go forward to grow forward. That has certainly been the case for me. Through my faith and upbringing, I've learned and carried this belief alongside lessons learned from my wrestling days and my time as an officer in the United States Army.

All my challenges and opportunities have taught me the importance of never accepting defeat and how vital it is to keep pushing and moving forward to stand up and win.

A large part of any business success is driven by showing up. That means showing up for meetings, for colleagues, for conferences. Keep showing up and going forward.

It's as simple and as powerful as that: just as I once learned on the wrestling mat, you must show up and get up on your feet if you get knocked down. That's the way you grow. Any defeat can be overcome; anything can be accomplished by creating that forward momentum.

In fact, by making the choice to stand up and go forward, you grow. *When you make the effort to go forward, you'll grow forward.* Growth is inevitable with the right mindset.

Make a Commitment to Show Up

Showing up means being present and committed. That commitment is something we fully embrace at my company Forge Business Solutions. As a business strategy company, we assist for-profit, nonprofit, government, and other organizations to develop their core business strategy. We help commercial clients develop the right methods to do business with the federal government, assist nonprofit organizations with growth strategies, and work to develop custom strategies that help companies achieve their specific goals.

Our business service is based on creating connections within communities. Using strategic planning, we work with companies to shape their objectives and create results.

Forge is headquartered in Morgantown, West Virginia, where I live with my wife and children. Forge is a certified veteran-owned small business, and we employ veterans and non-veterans alike. Some of our strong sense of service comes from the time we spent in the military and federal government.

Personally, my belief in the power of service began even before joining the Army and serving in the National Guard. Being class president of my high school, serving as a member of my community's local ambulance squad as a teenager, and participating in the sport of wrestling all reinforced that sense of commitment that Forge represents. Whatever goals a company may have, we facilitate achieving them.

Wrestling, the military, and my faith have each deeply impacted me, providing me with a strong sense of discipline, commitment, perseverance, and the importance of giving back. They have created a support network for me that has enabled me to take risks, push myself to try new things, and hold myself accountable. Each of these aspects of my life ensured that I didn't give up, take short cuts, or choose the wrong path, which are lessons that continue to stay with me today in my personal life, in my business life, and as a civic leader.

Business, like life, is all about progress and the willingness to go through tough times, rebuild if necessary, and stand right back up again. Regardless of the challenges we face, we're a lot stronger than we think we are.

In writing this book, my goal is to assist other business professionals and entrepreneurs in developing that same strength and resilience for themselves. I hope to share some of my own empowering lessons and how I have applied them.

Isn't it time you empowered your business and your life and made an impact on those around you?

Chapter 1

Showing Up

(Go to Grow)

Showing up accounts for 90% of anyone's business or personal success. In my own experience, this alone has provided me with so much of the fuel that powers both my business and personal aspirations.

It's a practice I learned early in life. My father passed away when I was 10, at a time when my family had limited means and opportunities. But as I grew older, by participating in wrestling and joining the military, many new experiences came about. Doors began to open, starting with my first airplane flight at age 17 to attend basic training, an experience I will never forget.

The more I discovered and took advantage of the opportunities presented to me by the military, the more opportunities I found, ultimately experiencing creative inspiration and the expansion of so many possibilities in my life. Meeting others from many cultures and ethnicities and being exposed to new people and new and diverse worlds furthered my growth, both then and now.

Being physically and actively present is your greatest advantage for discovering new opportunities in networking, career, and skill development.

Experience Shapes Your Decisions

Years before joining the Army, I had an opportunity to attend a special camp on the Princeton University campus, all expenses paid. It opened my eyes to new possibilities. Neither of my parents finished high school, and at the time, I assumed my adult life would be similar.

Opportunities make you who you are. But the first step is always showing up to experience them.

Experience shapes the way you make decisions and leads to the choices that are the most beneficial to you and your business.

To continue to grow, stepping outside your own comfort zone is essential. For example, my willingness to serve in the Army opened endless opportunities and limitless possibilities for me. Attending Princeton University for summer camp was not in my plans, but the experience instilled in me the idea of going to college.

Pushing yourself, going beyond the familiar, and trying new things is key for a successful future. Just as such experiences shaped me, exposing yourself to new opportunities will help shape both your business and you. That's the way to discover new talents and expand your possibilities.

Along the way, if you discover you're not talented at something, you can still learn to appreciate talent when you see it — because you've been exposed to it. You don't have to play tennis well to know when you're watching a good match, nor do you need to become a skilled painter to appreciate the masters of visual art. But you do have to see the art and attend that tennis match.

Almost any experience can be valuable, benefiting your growth or providing you with new opportunities. Having new experiences can make you more creative and resourceful. My own experiences have been a key factor in my business success.

In short, both personally and in business – showing up for experiences is how you grow.

Growing Your Business

New business opportunities arise when you show up and meet new people, and when you take on work that others aren't willing to do.

You need to do heavy lifting and make the effort to be better than your competition.

Growing a business depends on these three things:

- Being present
- Becoming exposed to new experiences and opportunities
- Having the willingness to invest time, talent, and treasure when you discover those opportunities

Remember, *when you show up, you're going to grow.* Accept the challenges that come your way and take your commitment to your business one step farther than anyone else will go to make an impact.

Make an Impact with a Personal Touch

In many cases, making an impact through your business starts with a small but important act of connecting with others. Connecting and forming relationships is vital for achieving success and knowledge in all areas of your life.

One way I connect is quite simple but surprisingly uncommon. I use a personal handwritten note.

After collecting business cards at meetings or conferences following an event, I'll send everyone I've met a note. If I meet the same person at several different locations, I'll write that person multiple notes. Making this small but important personal effort is all about building good personal relationships.

Writing that personal note is confirmation that someone is important to me. Going that extra step shows you're not just going through the motions; you're taking the time to show your appreciation for the experience of meeting that person.

Each of my notes are personalized. They aren't mass produced, and they don't say the same thing over and over. I make references to personal interactions and conversations. Each one is a message tailored to the person on the receiving end, and I've received a lot of positive feedback about them.

Making this kind of impact is important in whatever way you choose to do so. But remember, you can't create an impact at all if you don't go out there and have the experiences that provide the opportunity to be impactful.

Thinking and Stepping Outside the Box

One of the most important things that I encourage my clients to do is to think outside their own individual boxes and to step outside of them, too. It is essential to connect with people and understand them and their points of view, or even be willing to consider different perspectives.

Working as a business consultant and strategist, I'm not a subject matter expert on everyone's individual business. That said, I can introduce you to solutions you may not have considered. Providing information on how other organizations work and connecting clients with new resources and relationships in many different parts of the country is one vital part of our work at Forge. But the only reason that I can provide these connections is because I got on that first plane and made the effort to establish personal connections with a wide variety of people over time.

If you show up, you grow.

By being actively present in new experiences, you'll vastly increase your ability to uncover new opportunities to grow your career, your business, or yourself, developing new skills and new ways to learn.

The more you show up, the more you learn and the more your business will grow. Step outside your box and start growing!

"Efforts and courage are not enough without purpose and direction."

John F. Kennedy

<u>Takeaways</u>

- Do you actively pursue new opportunities?
    - Have you ever engaged in a new experience?
    - Was it difficult for you to do so?
    - Why or why not?
- What are some of the new perspectives you've gained from having new experiences?
- Have you stepped out of your comfort zone?
- Can you think of ways to make an impact on the people you meet?

Chapter 2

Going Above and Beyond

Going above and beyond in business means providing differentiated value. Your value is your worth. Differentiating that worth means that you exceed others' expectations and consistently work to build a strong professional and personal reputation. Being able to implement this in business and in life positions you as a high achiever: someone who can be relied upon to deliver exceptional results with purposeful direction.

Delivering Results

When you establish your differentiated value in a competitive environment, you're going above and beyond what your peers can provide. In fact, that's what sets you apart from them and gives you a competitive edge in both your career and your personal endeavors. You are delivering valuable results.

Whether it's a working relationship or a personal one, people are constantly seeking a service, and you can be the one to provide it. In some cases, that's exactly what you need to do. If someone asks you for directions, you don't need to lead them to their destination; just give them the information they asked for. If someone asks you for a drink, you hand them the drink; you don't explain the process of making the beverage.

However, to build a successful business, taking extra steps and providing additional information that can help others is what will differentiate you in a crowded marketplace. For example, if you anticipate and understand what another person is trying to achieve in the sense of a bigger picture, then you can act in a broader way. You can give them not only what they've asked for, but more than that. This is what shapes real differentiated value.

As an example of how we assist clients with strategic planning, through understanding their business needs, we will often realize there are introductions we can make to other resources that could serve as a conduit for their development. Perhaps we could introduce our client to legislators who can help support that client's industry or assist in passing a beneficial law. In part, this is why I became a registered lobbyist. If a business is growth-oriented and interested in expansion, perhaps we can connect them with a staffing firm that can assist with that business's skilled hiring needs. Maybe we will be able to introduce that client to a realtor who can provide expanded office space, or to the officials and advocates who could facilitate building new space on an existing site. Making these connections is a little step for us, but they are invaluable for our clients.

By exploring so many different relationships ourselves, we're able to offer greater connectivity to our clients. This not only assists our clients, but in turn differentiates our service because we provide opportunities that other businesses aren't offering.

Grow Through Differentiated Value

I've certainly experienced the benefits of differentiated value myself. When I attended Valley Forge Military College, I didn't just receive an education. I went to a military school that helped me identify, explore, and develop my strengths.

I didn't simply memorize facts and lessons in one class only to forget them as soon as I finished the final test. I received more than the information a class alone could provide and more than just a degree. With the kind of encouragement and development opportunities I was offered,

I became my college class president, as well as the regimental Sergeant Major of the Corps, which is a senior ranking cadet with a great deal of responsibility over the Corps.

Because I was introduced to the idea of a bigger picture by my school, with the sense of purpose inherent in expanding my own value to others, I put myself out there to run for class president and senior leader.

Sometimes reaching out in that way can be challenging. If you succeed, you may not want to take on that sort of responsibility or you may worry about failing. But reaching out no matter what happens is important. Nothing will happen — nothing will change — if you never take that action.

Because I saw great value in trying, I reached out to embrace those opportunities myself. Even though I was nervous about being rejected, I tried to reach for my goals. Being encouraged to make that reach was part of what I learned at Valley Forge and part of the commitment the school made to me. That's differentiated value.

If you don't succeed, dust yourself off, get up off the mat, and try again. I learned that in wrestling, at the Academy, and in the Army. This lesson had great value. You can't succeed if you don't try to go above and beyond the ordinary and expected; you must pursue your success and embrace the possibility of achievement even if there's a chance you won't be able to obtain it. That is how you grow.

Processing Failure

While I was successful with my college pursuits, I knew there was a possibility I would fail. Failing isn't easy for most people to accept. It certainly isn't easy for me.

Processing failure can be slow and painful, but it informs who you are. Your ability to accept the fact that you might fail is key. Keep trying and seeking and be resolved to do so. You must try, in other words, because without the possibility of failure, you have no chance of winning.

To quote Matthew 7,

"Ask and it will be given to you; seek and you will find; knock and the door will be opened to you. For everyone who asks receives; the one who seeks finds; and to the one who knocks, the door will be opened."

Seek first. If you do, you may not find exactly what you want, but you'll be shaped by the experience.

There's No Single Formula for Success

While there is no "one size fits all" mentality for any business or individual's success, and no single formula for providing differentiated value, it is still essential to set a pace for success. And once you've set that pace, lead others to keep up with you.

Forge is a company that is knowledge based. We sell our collective education, experiences, and expertise rather than manufacturing items or selling technology or equipment. We must set the pace for helping our clients grow as we have grown through our knowledge and experience. Setting that pace is a large part of how we go above and beyond with our business. It's our differentiated value.

Just as Aristotle said,

"The whole is greater than the sum of its parts."

Working together with our clients, as well as with our partners, we are stronger and more valuable than we would be on our own. We are more effective than we would be if we were working as individuals. We can accomplish more together than alone. We can set the pace for others to walk with us toward success.

"When you have exhausted all possibilities, remember this: you haven't."

Thomas A. Edison

Takeaways

- Have you ever been afraid of taking a big action?
    - If you took it anyway, what was the outcome?
    - Did you succeed or did you fail?
- Have you ever had to process failure?
    - Do you have a technique that you use to move past it or use it as a new starting point for success?
- Have you experienced differentiated value in businesses or personal relationships? What made you view these experiences as going "above and beyond?"

Chapter 3

Contributing At Your Best Level

"Gold medals aren't really made of gold. They're made of sweat, determination, and a hard-to-find alloy called guts."

Dan Gable

When you contribute at your best level, you identify your own strengths and the strengths of others. Just as my military service and college experiences helped me identify my own strengths, I know that as a business leader and mentor, I can help others recognize their strengths.

Any successful business leader must start by understanding their own skills and those of their team members.

While we can't all be highly skilled at everything we do, we each have key talents and values.

Recognizing that fact, as a leader, I can:

- Help foster growth and help others achieve success
- Identify and support other's goals and what they want to achieve

If you're putting a team together, and you allow everyone to contribute at their highest value, they'll enjoy making those contributions. They'll want to contribute more, and they'll want to become more successful at doing so.

That's why it's so essential to identify and support the strengths of the people on your team. By identifying them, you can make sure that you're building the right team: one where everyone complements each other rather than competing with or overriding each other.

Personally, I take pride in having people on my team who are smarter than I am at what they do, and whose contributions make us more talented and well-rounded .

Knowing Your Own Strengths

As renowned attorney Edward Bennet Williams Henry relayed in the book *The Man to See*,

"I may not know all the right answers, but I know who to call to get the answers."

I take a lot of pride in knowing people who can get the answers that people need to succeed.

My strength is in communicating and leading, and in identifying the right people and making the right connections. Leaning into your strengths is important: when you can identify your own strengths you can then successfully find and lean on others who are skilled in your weaker areas.

For example, I can't do plumbing, but I know the best plumber to call, and I can connect you with that person. I can't do graphic design for your website, but I know the right designers to call for your specific business type. That is the kind of knowledge that you should work on having both personally and for your business. Identify your skills and find others who can provide the skills that you don't have, both on and off your business team.

What I enjoy most about what I do for a living, and in my personal life as well, is helping people find the resources they need. Knowing the people who can provide the answers other people may need is one of the key strengths that I have to share. Similarly, no leader would be effective without knowing their own strengths.

Identifying the Goals of Others

One of the most enjoyable things about leadership is bringing a team together and accentuating the strengths of each member. Giving everyone the opportunity to grow, whether they are members of my team or my clients' teams, is not only personally rewarding for me, but also an important aspect of leading.

Of course, each person can only grow so much. None of us can double our capabilities and skills. But promoting the idea of success and helping each person to align their efforts with those of the organization or team they are a part of makes growth limitless.

For an example of this in action, look at the Navy SEALs. They're an elite military force. Each member is aligned as a part of a skilled team, a shared mission, and a long-term vision. Being members of a cohesive group means that each member can depend on the others. It's just as Aristotle said: the whole is greater than the sum of its parts.

As a leader, when you identify the goals of others and what they want to achieve, you can help each group member to achieve at their highest level. They can each be on the same page as to what they wish to achieve.

What's In it For Me?

Many people listen to what I call the WIFM Radio Station — "What's In it For Me."

But rather than focusing on only what appeals to or suits our needs, if we can identify and appeal to the vision of each member of a team, or to others in general, their engagement and commitment will increase. This leads to improvements in how often they succeed and how they are rewarded for their efforts. *A rewarded action is a repeated action.* This means that the more they succeed and reap the rewards, the more their positive actions will multiply exponentially.

As a leader it is essential to reward others when they've done good work. Personally, I know how great it feels to have a client tell me they're pleased with my work. When we get referrals telling us how well we did for an existing client, it's extremely validating and gratifying.

Don't you want those same feelings of gratification and validation for members of your team? Of course you do, because not only will those feelings make them enjoy their work and encourage further contribution, but they will also make your organization more successful overall. Recognition creates a positive culture for success in your company. By letting your team members know when they've done valuable work, you're encouraging them to contribute at their best level.

Establishing a Motivational Alignment

Another important aspect of leadership is to make certain that your team members are in the right roles. Consider your team's educational background, as well as the positions they have held in the past or aspire to hold in the future. It can also be useful to look at their interests outside of their professional lives.

Of course, with all of this in mind, you may not have the perfect role to fit an individual, at least not initially.

When you're running your own business, you often need to wear many different hats yourself. If you have limited resources, it's natural to expect others to wear all those hats, too, even if they may not fit perfectly.

Acknowledging that a job may not be a perfect fit for a team member is key. Let the person know that you appreciate them taking on a role that may be outside their comfort zone. That recognition is important. It's a way of expressing appreciation for their efforts, even if you know they're not doing the work that's best for them to do.

That expression of gratitude will encourage their best effort and help to prevent dissatisfaction or disengagement. Of course, at some point, when you value your team members, you will need to make sure you have or can create a role that will suit them better, or you'll risk losing them. No one wants to continue doing work that they aren't suited for forever.

As a leader, when you're working with people and asking them to do things that they may not have the highest level of motivational alignment for, it's imperative to:

- Identify that you're aware of the situation
- Let your team member know you're asking them to do something that may not be their ideal role
- Work to provide a timeline for when they can move into a role more suitable for them

Most people will be more accommodating of being asked to do tasks that fall outside their "sweet spot" if they know you're aware of this and working to find a more optimal solution.

Of course, even if you have a role a team member is fully qualified for and has expressed interest in, sometimes you may find that a team member is simply not suited for a specific position. On the other hand, if they're operating well at a position that they're good at, then you've placed them where they align in terms of both their skills and motivation.

So exactly how do you determine a good alignment?

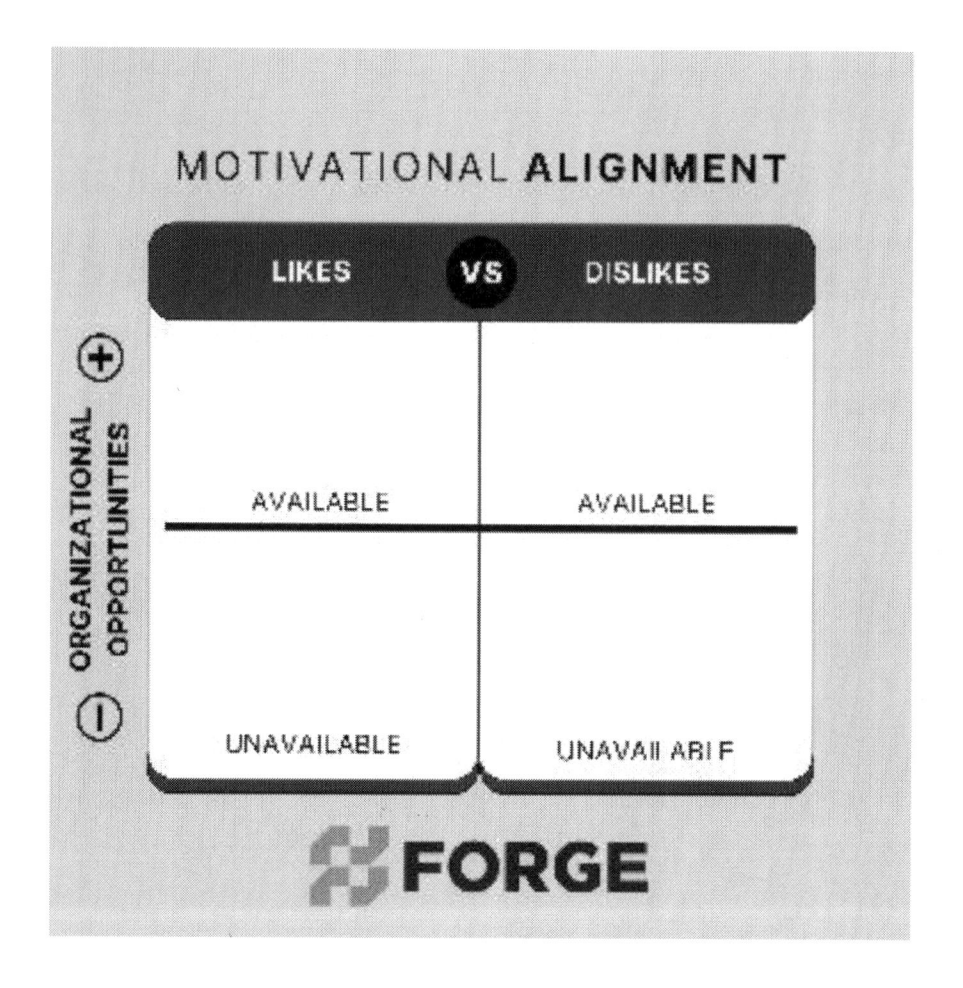

Using a Quadrant Approach

MOTIVATIONAL ALIGNMENT

LIKES VS DISLIKES

ORGANIZATIONAL OPPORTUNITIES (+/−)

| AVAILABLE | AVAILABLE |
| UNAVAILABLE | UNAVAILABLE |

FORGE

One good way to determine motivational alignment is by using a quadrant approach. It's not complicated: simply draw a quadrant — four boxes — broken into sections that identify each team member's:

- Likes
- Dislikes

- Organizational opportunities that are available
- Organizational opportunities that are unavailable

Look at the intersection of each of those areas. Obviously, if something is disliked and it's *not* part of the job someone is required to do, it doesn't matter. It is irrelevant to the position at hand. On the other hand, if there is something that one of your team members doesn't like, but it *is* part of their job, determine how much of that activity they'll have to do regularly. Is it something that they can become motivated to accomplish and be successful at achieving? Or is it something that you are aware they will never become adept at accomplishing?

Next look at the quadrant that represents the things you know your team member *likes to do*. Consider how many of those areas will make up a regular part of the position. Ideally, that's where you want most of their responsibilities to be.

Remember, too, that if there are things they really like, and are good at, but are *not* part of the job they are doing, they will very likely seek a role elsewhere that *does include* their main interests and capabilities.

Your next step should be to go over the core duties of a position or a project. Place those duties into the four separate quadrants indicating likes, dislikes, the duties that are and are not a part of a job. You'll be able to see where the individual you're thinking of for that opportunity will line up. Do most of their capabilities and interests fit into the likes and duties quadrants? Or is the job primarily made up of areas where your prospective team member is not qualified or actively dislikes handling the responsibilities required to succeed at the position?

Using the tool of four quadrants is an excellent way to determine motivational fit.

Ask Questions

Of course, along with using a quadrant approach, if you're not already familiar with a person's skills, likes, and dislikes, then you should ask some questions to determine them.

Ask your team member:

- What do you like to do?
- What do you like best about your position?
- What do you dislike?

Working conditions should be taken into consideration as well as the duties involved in a position. For example, consider whether an individual prefers to be left alone undisturbed to do their work, or whether they are most motivated by working in a group. The same duties can be ideal for one person in one type of setting and detrimental for another person in a different setting.

A skilled accountant might prefer to work in a quiet office, or they may enjoy working as part of a team with other members of a financial department. While one individual might enjoy creating presentations if they can work privately to conceptualize them away from other distractions, another team member might function best by creating a presentation with the input of others, working in a busy setting.

Finding the right fit for your team in terms of workspace as well as their backgrounds and job duties will drive their innovation and creativity. It will go a long way toward encouraging them to introduce new ideas and perspectives and achieve at their highest levels for their own good and that of the organization.

Successful motivation and placement all starts with identifying when, where, and how they are going to be successful and how you can help them to be and stay motivated.

Create A Positive Ripple Effect

While managing your team is an important task for any leader, your own commitment to performing your best is important, too. When you're performing at your highest level, you can inspire and motivate others to elevate their contributions and create a positive, productive team dynamic.

Remember, we all want to be a part of something, so as a leader, it is also your responsibility to foster a sense of human connection. When people become disenfranchised, it will hamper their performance. It's always important to encourage connectivity and engagement.

If a person feels forgotten or disregarded, or they don't feel that they're a part of the company's greater good, they'll become disengaged. Each team member should feel that they are a valued part of the team effort. Unfortunately, in many organizations, that is not the case.

In fact, recent studies have shown that more than 70% of employees are disengaged from their work. They feel alienated from their organization's goals and ideals. Naturally, that creates job dissatisfaction which impacts productivity. It interferes in their alignment with their work. If people feel their work is unimportant or not valued, they begin to disconnect from the rest of the team. They will start to back off until they eventually walk away from their work all together.

It's not unlike being part of a wrestling team. If your effort is not appreciated, you'll start to pull back here and there. You may start skipping practices. And then finally, you may believe you're no longer a part of the team. You may believe no one cares if you're there or not.

As a leader, if you're not engaging with your organization's team and making certain that they feel valued, there's danger ahead. You may lose team members or find the organization's productivity has nose-dived with that type of leadership. That type of leadership puts you at risk of a negative spiral for the organization. Thankfully, the opposite is true if you can create a positive ripple effect throughout your organization.

How do you do that?

- Give feedback
- Provide valid public praise
- Provide constructive criticism privately
- Create a culture of positivity and a work environment that suits your team members

If you're not actively creating the right work environment and providing feedback, then you can't expect your team members to be active either.

Be Specific with Praise and Criticism

Providing praise and criticism are both essential for boosting your team members' achievements. But providing vague generalities is not enough. It's vital to be specific with both your praise and criticism.

Don't simply tell people that they're doing a good job and toss out random superlatives. Instead, let the person know that they did great work on a specific project, and share why you feel that way. Tell them what they did right in detail. Let them know that you're aware of their efforts. People appreciate your acknowledgement and your attention.

Speaking personally, when you tell me something about my work that is specific, I know you care about me and you're engaging with what I do. This establishes human connection, which encourages your team to contribute at their best and highest levels. That connection creates an environment where you can provide your team members with a sense of purpose.

On the other hand, if you say something general and rote like "good job," you're not providing any worthwhile feedback or engagement.

Regarding criticism, you should also be specific. Point out specific areas that need improvement, rather than offering some general assessment that something is unacceptable or needs to be reconsidered. Criticism, unlike praise, should be presented privately. And when applied constructively, don't forget to reward your team members for making the change or improvement.

The Importance of Belonging

By understanding your team members' educations, experiences, and backgrounds, you'll be able to determine the right roles and responsibilities — the best alignment and motivational fit — for each member of your team. Your connections through praise and constructive criticism will help you to create a positive ripple effect that will give you and your organization the best opportunities for success. You will also be encouraging your team members to think they are a good fit for your organization and will establish a sense of belonging.

That establishment is key. We all want to be a part of something bigger than ourselves. I've been fortunate enough to serve on the boards of many volunteer organizations. Just about everyone who comes to work for or with those organizations does so to spread more positive change in the world. At least initially, they share a sense of belonging, a sense of purpose.

But people don't always stay in these positions. Many feel underappreciated. They don't see themselves as integral to that organization.

In a volunteer-based organization – or in any business organization – it's important to find out what a person enjoys doing, place them where they can do what they enjoy, and *give them the opportunity to really contribute their talents and time.*

Regardless of the position, it's always best to put people where they *want* to be, not just where you *need* them to be. Give them that important sense of belonging.

For small business owners, this is especially vital. Entrepreneurs need to go above and beyond to make certain their team members know they're celebrated and not merely tolerated.

If you've done a thorough job of determining a person's motivational alignment, when the individual does their work and does it well, that should always be celebrated.

Don't you want to be where you're celebrated for your achievements and where others appreciate who you are and your engagement? Don't you prefer that over struggling to be someone or something you're not? I know that I want to be where people appreciate who I am and the skills and services I can share with them.

As an employer and a leader, it's imperative for you to understand your team members and create that celebratory environment for them.

These are the tools you need to evaluate your employees:

- **Discover** who they are and find their best motivational alignment

- **Explore** what motivates them
- **Build** their sense of purpose by encouraging and celebrating them
- **Deploy** them in ways that encourage their growth and their highest level of contribution, which will lead to future successes

When you discover, explore, build, and deploy your team well, then you're operating at your best level as a leader, too.

"The strength of the team is each individual member. The strength of each member is the team."

Phil Jackson

Takeaways

- Have you helped foster the growth of others and identified what they want to achieve?
    - Have you identified what you want to achieve?
- Can you think of any times when you've felt a strong sense of belonging?
    - What made you feel that way?
- Have you examined the motivational alignment of your team members? What about your own?
    - Can you describe what motivates you?

- Can you help your team members find the projects or jobs that will fit them the best?

Chapter 4

Waste Nothing

We've talked about establishing tools for the success of your organization and your team members. But what about those times when, even though you may have tried to the best of your ability, things don't work out as planned?

Everything in life is a lesson. Everyone experiences some failures in life and in business. Don't waste the lessons you can learn from those situations.

Failing is not a loss, it's a lesson. Unlike school, where you are taught certain facts and lessons and then tested on your knowledge, life presents a different kind of test. *Life tests first and teaches second.*

In life, it's important not to skip over any mistakes. Don't just dust yourself off and push that mistake aside, forgetting about it. If you do so, you could waste an important opportunity. You could miss a chance to truly learn from and grow from your mistake or failure. Waste nothing! I can't stress that enough.

My entire life has been a cycle. I've climbed out of various difficult situations. I've made mistakes and I've faced adversity. After my father passed away, I had to climb my way out. My parents weren't college educated but they worked hard and taught me to do the same. I aspired to climb to the next level. If anything, the adversity of my background is what helped inspire me to achieve more than I might have been able to if I had come from a different family situation.

Use Adversity to Improve

Adversity often leads to opportunity. I could have missed some of the best opportunities I've experienced in my life if there wasn't some level of adversity for me to overcome first.

One of the best pieces of advice I can give you in business and life is this:

Don't waste difficulty and adversity when they arise.

Instead, use them as tools. Use them to become even better, getting back on your feet and demonstrating that you can score from the bottom – just as you can score from the bottom in wrestling, reversing your position. Push your way back onto your feet. Use what you learned when you were down to keep rising.

Even though we often think that we are fully in control of our lives, we're not. Being humble enough to use adversity to gain control of our narratives again is an important technique for both survival and success.

I started working 40 hours a week as a laborer at an apartment complex. My grandfather was the maintenance person at the complex and helped me get hired. I was working hard and paying taxes at the age of 14. It wasn't what my friends from school were doing that summer and it wasn't necessarily what I wanted to do. It was difficult, and I didn't love it, but I used that work situation to help my family. It helped shape me in a positive way. The level of intense physical labor made me stronger physically and mentally.

When I joined the military at 17, and then when I started my first civilian job, there were other challenges to face, and other mistakes to make. Through it all, I have consistently tried to be a good son, brother, husband, and father.

Embrace the Suck

Despite my good intentions, I haven't always been successful. But because my personal vision and my faith are aligned, I was able to move through any failure. It has been a strong compass for me in business and in all aspects of my life that when facing any failure, I can return to my faith. That's my true north. No matter what happens, my faith can guide me through even the most difficult lessons in life.

Of course, it's human nature to want to get back on your feet and eradicate your failures, pretending they never happened. However, we must be careful not to move too fast, because it's important for us to learn from our mistakes, not to just try and erase them.

Instead, embrace the suck!

- Learn from your mistakes
- Get comfortable with being uncomfortable, because that is how you'll grow as a person and gain strength as well as wisdom
- Don't be afraid to take responsibility for your mistakes and acknowledge them
- Keep moving forward

You'll find that when you do, people will respect and even reward you for taking responsibility for your mistakes instead of attempting to sweep them under the rug as soon as possible.

When a mistake or failure happens, consider what it can teach you, and then keep moving forward, strengthened by the knowledge you've gained. Even if you feel like just hunkering down, pulling a blanket up over your head and hiding, or your instinct is to come to a full a stop when you do something that you regret, remember – don't waste the low point you're in. Don't waste your time in the valley. Use it, gain from it, and keep going.

In wrestling, your time on the bottom is a defensive position, not an offensive one. Yet that is the time when it's most critical to score – from the bottom.

But the importance of scoring from the bottom is true not only in wrestling but in business and throughout your life. Use the weight of the world that's upon you. Use that pressure to put in the greatest effort, stand up, and score again.

Of course, to stand up and score, you must start in that defensive position and use the momentum of all that's pressing against you. Using that weight and that momentum is how you'll rise above your current situation, whatever it may be.

Scoring from the bottom in that way is especially meaningful. That's how you build your confidence. Once you've achieved something even while in that position, you'll know that whenever you experience a challenge in the future, whenever you're down, you can learn and strategize from your position, move into action, and get right back up again.

When you find a way to get up and score from the bottom, your momentum is leveled up even higher.

The action of scoring from the bottom makes you think differently about getting up again the next time you're down. You'll know you can do it no matter what happens. You can score a win, even when defeat seems imminent.

It's true that it's not simple or easy to get up. But once you learn that you can do it, you will do it again and again.

It all starts with creating a strategy to do so:

- Figure out where you are
- Understand your circumstances
- Identify your resources
- Become uncomfortable
- Push your way up despite the pressure weighing against you

Once you have successfully faced that pressure, and used it to stand up again, you'll find that you are stronger than ever before. Just as diamonds are shaped and strengthened through pressure, so are you.

Failure Isn't Fatal

Don't think of failure as a permanent state. Failure can encourage you to rise again and gain the strength you need to win again. It also leads to humility that will help you to build connections with other people. You'll find that many others will see their own struggles and challenges in your stories. Whether they are inspired by them or recognize how your experiences parallel their own, humility connects us all.

One of the things that I hope this book will do is inspire others to recognize and face adversity, and use their mistakes, their failures, and their perceived failures for good.

In Romans, 8:28, scripture says that *all things come together for our good* – not that all good things come together for us. The challenges you face, the adversities you overcome, serve to bring you together with others and connect you with others in honesty and humility. If you're able to learn from and express your own mistakes, others will relate to you. It makes you truly humble and people relate to that humility. We all make mistakes, and it's fine to acknowledge and commiserate over them, even if we don't always post them on Facebook.

Mistakes and failures are just two elements in your life. It's all part of the mix. Think of all the elements in your life as you would the ingredients in making a batch of cookies. Eggs and flour may be part of the recipe, but eating a raw egg or a spoonful of flour on its own isn't going to taste great. Sure, eating a handful of chocolate chips or a spoonful of sugar could be enjoyable, but neither will taste as delicious as when you mix them with the flour, egg, sugar, and shortening necessary to create a cookie. When you mix all those different elements together, that's the recipe for success.

Our lives are no different. We mix different elements together for the best outcome. In life, those elements include mistakes made and challenges faced, and all the adversity that must be overcome. They include humility and honesty in sharing our own failures.

Remember, failure isn't fatal. But it does take a great deal of character to go out there and try again after a defeat. When you do, others will respect you for your effort.

I have a picture I treasure of my son. In it, he's raising his hand at a wrestling match even though he was brokenhearted about a previous loss. He was still committed to going out there again and wrestling the last match of the day. He had the courage to do so, even though he knew at that point that he would not place in the tournament. He faced the challenge with courage. Admitting your failures and going back out there even after you've been defeated builds character and helps you connect with others and be a more effective and influential leader.

Lessons Not Losses

Don't forget that there are no real losses in life, only lessons. But it's entirely up to you to define adversity in that way. It's your choice to decide if you're going to let a challenge become a loss or a lesson.

Let nothing go to waste. Certainly, no failure is wasted if we learn from it. Remember that life tests us first and then teaches us second – if we only allow it to do so.

If you're not failing, it means you're not trying.

It's okay to fail if you try. We live in a society dominated by social media success stories and seemingly picture-perfect lives. But that's not reality. The reality is that there will always be lessons to learn, valleys to climb out of, and spectacular views from the top of the mountain.

Openly Learn from and Admit Mistakes

In business, wasting nothing means learning actively and admitting to your mistakes. Doing so increases your credibility and builds trust with others. It shows humility and a commitment to improvement. Analyzing and understanding your mistakes improves your problem-solving skills and leads to more effective solutions in the future. There is nothing wasted from embracing and accepting failures and learning from them.

In your organization, it's important to create a culture that acknowledges lessons to be learned. This is the type of culture that will encourage productivity and creativity – even if the result is not always successful.

As a leader, it's important to foster and reward creative behavior because that's the way you'll find new solutions. Take the risks that you need to take or encourage others to take and accept the lessons you learn along the way. That's the right path to follow for meeting the needs of your customers and creating growth for your organization.

"And we know that all things work together for good ..."

Romans 8:28

Takeaways

- Have you learned the difference between lessons and losses?
- Do you learn from and admit your mistakes?
- How can you improve your problem-solving abilities?

- When you openly admit mistakes, what do you find is the result of this acceptance? Can you describe what has occurred for you in the past?

Chapter 5

Don't Be a Victim

"Success is how high you bounce when you hit bottom."

George S. Patton

Just as it's important to think of life and business in terms of lessons learned instead of losses, it's equally vital to understand that acting or thinking like a victim does no good at all.

Painting yourself as a victim is one of the worst things that you can do in business. It is the complete opposite of accepting and learning from your mistakes.

The solution is to *eliminate even the idea of making excuses in your life.*

- Do everything that you can do
- Be proactive
- Own your actions and be resourceful
- Never make excuses – there is nothing to be gained from expressing sentiments like "I couldn't because no one told me…I didn't hear about that…They never called me back."
- Refuse to be a victim

Promote Proactivity and Empowerment

When you refuse to be a victim, you're taking a proactive stance in life. You're focusing on what you can control and change rather than feeling helpless or blaming external factors for the challenges you face.

In business, it is important to be a victor rather than a victim.

As Winston Churchill once said,

"History will be kind to me for I intend to write it."

When you write your own story, you take what appears to be an obstacle or a defeat and use it to become better and stronger, which is the lesson I learned in wrestling. If you simply accept defeat, then you're embracing that victim mentality.

Instead, embrace the opportunities that are ahead of you. Keep a positive attitude about the challenges you face rather than taking on the mentality of a victim. Promote proactivity throughout your organization – it will empower others as well as empower you.

In other words, if you didn't hear about an event or an opportunity to bid on a project, then find the information you need. If it's too late to get in under the wire this time, then be sure you're on the list for notification of these events or opportunities the next time.

On countless occasions, I've called organizations and asked to be added to an invitation list so I can attend events that may help me grow my business. It's not difficult to do. Just make that connection and follow up to be sure it's been made.

Your business and life itself are not spectator sports. Instead, you must get out there and go all in for what you need and want.

Reaching the Mountain Summit

Think of challenges this way: you can't reach the mountain summit if you've never been in the valley. This is a theme I keep returning to. The lessons you learn in the valley are what will propel you to reach the heights.

If something doesn't go the way you thought it would, don't complain and say, "This happened to me." Instead, reframe whatever occurred and say, "This happened *for* me."

Whatever occurs, remember, you can most assuredly learn from it and become better. Instead of being the victim, use your time in that valley to propel you forward. Prepare to climb up to the next level of the mountain.

Enhance Your Problem-Solving Skills

Having a victim mindset in your career, your business, or your personal life is handing your power away. When you reject victimhood, you're more likely to engage in effective problem-solving, seeking solutions and alternatives rather than dwelling on the problem or unfairness of a situation.

As Henry Ford once said,

"Whether you think you can or you can't, you're right."

So, start thinking that you *can*.

If your mindset is that things are going to happen *to* you all day, why even get out of bed in the morning? By taking charge of your life and circumstances, you'll find that your self-esteem and confidence will get a big boost. You'll grow to recognize your own agency and ability to impact your life.

When you take control, you'll feel empowered. When you're empowered, you'll find that things are happening *for* you, not *to* you. Based on the wind, you can adjust your sails so to speak. Now of course the wind isn't going to blow your way every single day. But when you empower yourself to act, you can respond successfully to that wind. Trim the sails and don't miss the changes in direction.

Many businesses experience a sudden change in projects. Perhaps the current objective will get re-envisioned or postponed. If a project changes, it doesn't mean you're a victim of circumstance or a loser. It simply means that things have changed. Sometimes they do.

Learning the lessons that you need to empower yourself will lead you to enhance your problem-solving skills. You'll find ways to adjust to meet the challenges that inevitably arise in any life and in any business. You'll find that you will become more resourceful and more capable of solving problems.

How to Score

One of the key lessons you learn in business is how to score successes. I approach this idea as a wrestler and wrestling coach, thinking strategically about both how to score and how I can use whatever position I am in now to be better. Once you start problem solving in that strategic way, you'll achieve a level of confidence you didn't have before.

In wrestling, when you fall behind in the score, a victim simply gives up. But if you think strategically about improving your position and you are successful at it, your confidence grows abundantly.

Once you've proven you can come from behind and overcome a difficult situation, you'll feel energized to do it again. While you might wish you never had such situations to overcome, would you really want to be just sitting on top all the time, waiting for someone else to knock you from your position?

Personally, I enjoy being the underdog and having something to prove. The underdog isn't a victim; the underdog is the one who can solve any situation, take on adversity, and come from behind.

Fighter Mike Tyson once said,

> *"Everybody has a great plan until they get punched in the face."*

In business, it's important to be able to take a punch and still get up on your feet again. Once you do, you'll have learned how to avoid a punch next time. You learn more through taking on this kind of loss than through a constant stream of success. If there were never any challenges to face in your business, it would be extremely difficult to deal with one when it arrived.

When I was coaching a recent wrestling match, after losing the match, I told our student wrestlers that they just learned an important life lesson. As I've said in this book, in school you learn a lesson and then you're tested. But in life, you're tested first, and that's what teaches us lessons. We learn, and then we can do better the next time.

Empower Your People

Just as critical as empowering yourself and eschewing the mindset of a victim is empowering your team to do well, too. Setting a good example is key, but you should also be encouraging their productivity by stressing their ability to control their own destiny. You can help your team to do so by allowing them to have input on their own work and their conceptualization of their roles in your organization.

Using this approach can also assist with client projects as well. Our company worked on an organizational strategic plan with a local government agency. As we developed the project, we recognized that the organization's leaders were extremely intelligent and had many ideas of their own that weren't being fully engaged. We determined that there were ways we could engage them and allow them to facilitate their own strategies. We invited them to express their own needs and explore future opportunities. By empowering them, we could successfully collaborate with these leaders to shape a strategic plan for the entire organization.

In other situations, whether with your clients or with your own team members, creating a climate of empowerment goes hand in hand with learning how to eliminate a victim mindset. You're effectively shaping an environment where actions are encouraged and empowered, and where new solutions are considered.

Another of our recent clients at Forge had operated successfully as a commercial company for many years. Our goal was to help them build a business development plan to assist with acquiring federal and state government contracts.

Federal and state contracting is a far different environment than commercial business. In that context, their business model needed to transition to achieve success.

While we were able to help facilitate their transition, it was crucial that their team develop a proactive approach that's essential with government contracting. They could not be passive or allow themselves to fall into a victim mentality, waiting for calls that would not arrive. In these specific contracting spaces, follow-up and engagement are crucial, and putting in that type of effort is expected and necessary.

Bolstering Self-Esteem and Confidence with 72-Hour Rule

One good way of bolstering self-esteem in any business situation is what we call our 72-hour rule. If you haven't heard back from someone after 72 hours (three days), then it's time to make a call.

Why do we use this timeline?

- We are staying proactive and engaging others without pestering them
- We are reaching out to engage rather than waiting around and becoming a victim because we waited too long
- We are staying aware that sometimes people simply forget to get back to you and will be grateful for contact to remind them – as long as you're not bothering them too often or too soon

We're frequently overwhelmed with an onslaught of information every day. Personally, I find that it's common to get buried in it. I appreciate it when someone sends me an email or gives me a quick call as a reminder. But timing is still key. You do not want to become that company that's "always calling."

Changing Your Mindset

The first step in not falling prey to a victim mentality is to change your mindset. Remember that being tested in life teaches you a lesson. It doesn't teach you to be a victim.

When you have a setback, change your mindset. Look at whatever occurred as a set-up for greater things to come. Once you learn from that lesson, you'll prevent yourself or your organization from repeating it, and you'll also do better next time.

__Takeaways__

- Have you ever felt like the world was against you? How did you talk yourself out of that mindset – or did you?
- Are you using life's lessons to empower your future, or are you falling prey to the belief that you're powerless?
- Can you think of a way you can help to empower others on your team?
- Do you have a timeline for follow up with clients and potential clients? What is it and why? If you don't have one, why not?

Chapter 6

Learning to Train, Visualize, and Execute

My own positive mindset and my ability to get back on my feet again are both learned from my experience as a wrestler and a coach. I can train, visualize, and execute the wins I desire in my life, and abilities are all deeply rooted in the sport of wrestling. I owe my involvement in the sport to my best friend Eric, who introduced me to it over thirty years ago.

Wrestling, like my faith and my service in the military, has served as a guide on how to conduct my life and my business. It has taught me to train hard, to visualize my success, and to execute the outcomes I envisioned, all of which are important in achieving business success.

Regular training in the sport of wrestling combined with visualization techniques has significantly elevated my confidence and reduced anxiety, particularly in high-pressure situations.

Finding Purpose

Before I started wrestling, I didn't have a real purpose in my life. I was a kid who attended school, played, did homework, had dinner, and went to bed.

Although I had no long-term goals, I did develop a strong work ethic which I learned from my parents. My mother was a terrific cook and kept an immaculate home; she fully supported her three children every hour of the day. Before my father passed away, he held multiple jobs, working for 7-Up Bottling Company, delivering milk, and serving as a police officer in our community.

Observing their commitment and work ethic gave me the ability to undertake a physically challenging sport and thrive at it. I applied my observation of my parents' work ethic to my commitment to wrestling. I discovered that the harder I worked at learning wrestling, the quicker my learning became, and the more successes I began to achieve on the mat.

I leaned into my commitment and successes and tried even harder. I picked up running to improve my conditioning so I could last longer in the match and be stronger and more physical with my opponent. I studied technique because being more technical and more flexible allowed me to counter my opponents moves and set my attacks.

With each success my confidence was boosted. Because my achievements directly correlated to hard work, I worked harder. If I didn't give my all to practice, if I didn't work hard to get in better shape and make weight, then I couldn't succeed on the mat.

The more successes I had, the less anxious I felt. I saw the fruits of my hard work as my skills improved and my successes increased every year.

Increased Success Rate

The same methodical approach I applied toward succeeding at wrestling when I was younger led to a higher success rate for me throughout my life. I use the same combination of both physical preparation and mental readiness to execute whatever task I am facing.

The attitude I held toward wrestling moved into my attitude toward academics. Having struggled with diagnosed dyslexia, I had been a very average student, but my study habits and my successes academically began to improve.

If you don't learn and act upon the valuable correlation between hard work and success, you are just drifting through your life without having a real goal to work for. It's difficult if not impossible to achieve any success without working for it.

Recognizing the direct correlation between preparation and hard work to success has led me to achieve my own success and find a real sense of purpose – in wrestling, in service, and in my work.

Find Your Own Direction

Everyone needs a taste of success. Everyone needs to find something they're good at. Wrestling was how I first tasted success. I learned how to give everything I had to a match and improve my abilities every season.

Our son is in his freshman year in high school, and he wrestles now. He works hard both at the sport and academically, and he is starting to put the pieces together, enjoying the hard work he must undertake because he likes the successes that it creates. He has a goal; he's found a direction.

Along with that sense of direction, he's learned to be disciplined, to self-motivate and actualize. He has discovered how to achieve his goals without counting on anyone else to do the heavy lifting. Instead, he's learning how to carry that weight himself. These are skills that will serve him well throughout his life. Our twin daughters are experiencing these same lessons — one in softball and the other in basketball. Regardless of the sport, the lessons it teaches remain the same: be dedicated, be disciplined, and don't expect others to do the work for you.

Having that direction and that discipline is critical in both the world of business and in your personal life.

Discipline Is Key

Discipline is what motivates you when no one else is watching or holding you accountable. It is one of the foundations of running a successful business. There is always something to manage and some work to do. If you are not disciplined about individual tasks and your overall approach to business, it's difficult to become successful.

One of my first experiences with discipline was as a wrestler when I had to cut weight. That's a difficult thing to do, but to achieve that, after I got home from practice, I'd take a run before bed. There was no coach telling me I had to do that; I just did it to achieve my goal.

Although no one was watching me to see if I did it, the results spoke for themselves when I stepped on the scale. There was concrete evidence of the success of my discipline, just as I notice the evidence of a disciplined business today.

Without that sense of discipline, it can be difficult to succeed – whether on the mat or in business. I've seen many businesses fail because of a lack of discipline. The owner would be out golfing instead of going into the office every day.

Those business owners will soon learn what I was fortunate enough to pick up in the wrestling room: that without discipline, failure is guaranteed. That said, I also learned that failure isn't fun, but as I've stressed, it's not fatal. No matter how hard I worked, sometimes I would still get beat. The solution is to get back on your feet and get the next win.

That's still true today of course. Sometimes in our business, we put proposals together which we expect to be successful. All the same, our company doesn't always get every contract. I don't let that defeat be a setback for us. Instead, the next day, I'll come back more determined than ever that we will get the next opportunity.

That commitment to keep trying and not feel defeated is a tone I set for our team as well as myself. After all, we are all in the same boat together, figuratively speaking. The whole is greater than the sum of its parts. We all need to stay positive and work together for success. These are techniques that I learned first from wrestling and in the Army.

Who You Become in Private Becomes Who You Are in Public

With wrestling, and throughout my life, I've learned that who you are in private is who you will appear as in public.

Adding your small wins together and being able to get back up when you're down and score from the bottom is the key to your success.

I've had failures – honestly, more than I have had successes over time. But the important thing is that when you fail, you need to get back up again.

When you're down, that's the time you need to score. It may feel good to get the next business deal when things are already going well, but what really demonstrates your integrity and character is getting back up and trying again after you've been told no.

When you can turn the tide from losing a match to winning, just like the Kansas City Chiefs did in the 2024 Super Bowl, there's a deeper value in that. You know you can come from behind. You know that when things get rough you can still achieve your goal. Having the confidence to score when the odds are against you is how you succeed in business and throughout your life.

Wrestlers understand the importance of going hard for the full six minutes. As a coach, when I send a wrestler out to compete, I always tell them, "Give me the entire six minutes." I let them know that I am not focused on the score, and it doesn't matter if you get behind. Wrestle the entire time, and everything else will fall into place.

I learned the importance of not giving in and staying on the mat from wrestling, and I have applied that lesson throughout my life. Wrestling led me to the Army. My time in the military led me to do other work that I would not have done because it seemed impossible. But through wrestling, I learned that dedication pays off.

If you don't keep pushing, you can't ensure victory. For me, the thrill of getting a win is a motivator. So even if I didn't win at a meet or tournament, I'd try to create a win somewhere else, just to stay focused on my goal. If I had a tough day at wrestling, I would often go home and take a run, giving myself a win in that way. I still use that motivational trick when I've had a hard day at the office.

Remember, you are your biggest opponent. Don't let others – or your mindset – determine your victory. If you want to be the best, you must compete with the best – in wrestling and in business. Don't be afraid of the battle. Don't try to avoid the challenges.

In Proverbs 27:17 it's said that,

"As iron sharpens iron, so one person sharpens another."

To achieve more and to improve yourself, you'll find that being challenged will help you be better, and that there is even more benefit for continuing to improve yourself by helping others, mentoring, and providing leadership.

With the proper strategy and planning, you can ensure that every step you take in life is purposeful and directed toward a specific goal. That will help you determine what success looks like and what winning means to you. And no matter where you are on the mat, your life, or your business, believe in yourself and know that you hold the keys to victory.

Takeaways

- Have you ever given your all to something and tasted success from it?
- Do you take purposeful steps toward a strategic goal?
- Can you think of some examples of when you came out from behind to win at an activity, sport, or in business?
    - If so, how could you apply some of this same spirit in everyday life?
    - How do you determine what a "win" is and what success looks like?

Chapter 7

Service

"Everyone can be great, because everyone can serve."

Martin Luther King Jr.

Service is a value that I hold close to my heart. It's important to serve our country, our communities, members of our business teams, and our families. Mentoring others and providing knowledge and connections are integral parts of a life of service.

I enlisted in the Army and later served as a commissioned officer. I have served on the boards of multiple non-profits.

I fully believe in the words that President John F. Kennedy spoke during his inauguration speech:

> *"Ask not what your country can do for you, ask what you can do for your country."*

My belief is that we learn a lot from being in service to others. Investing our time, our talent, and treasure into our communities is one way to serve, and it is an excellent idea for businesses that are local or have local offices to give back at the community level as well. In the same way that you assist others, you may very well find that the community assists and supports you and your business success.

Speaking personally, I've served as chairman of our regional United Way, chaired multiple university boards, sat on visiting committees and tech industry boards, and served as chairman of the Chamber of Commerce board of directors. I was also honored to receive an appointment from the governor of West Virginia to the State Board of Education. Today, I serve as president of an angel investment board and network. I also sit on the board of our local Salvation Army.

As much if not more than I've served others, my service engagements have served me! I've always grown from these engagements, and from the relationships I've developed with the intelligent and generously caring people who serve beside me.

Those relationships are a return on my investment of time and knowledge from a business perspective, too. Giving back is important in and of itself of course, for the good of your community. But it also promotes goodwill and the message that you're a good corporate citizen. It shows you don't just take from your community and its people. It shows you're also willing and able to give back.

As a leader, I think it is also important to encourage your employees to give back. I encourage our team to be part of the local United Way campaign for example, and as a company, we work on projects that can benefit the community, veterans, students, and others in need.

Along with helping others outside your organization, encouraging this kind of endeavor also facilitates team building. Being of service creates a good, positive work culture, showing your employees and their families that you care about more than just profit. You care about the community, and through that, you care for your team as well.

In short, service:

- Helps your community
- Helps foster business connections
- Helps with team building
- Shows you care

You'll find that serving others is a win/win. It can introduce you to people you may not have connected with in any other way and help you grow your business. Additionally, being of service to others allows you to do good things that benefit your community, state, and country as well as your business. For your business to thrive, you want the community around you to thrive, too, after all.

Service creates a positive ripple effect, as you lead by example. Your team sees you give and contribute, which will encourage them to do the same; it benefits your company, your company culture, and the community that supports your business.

Service Helps You Find Purpose

As for me, I simply enjoy serving. While there are so many benefits from service, it's the act itself that I find the most worthwhile and fulfilling.

Serving allows you to do good for others while building a bigger business network for your own organization. It creates the ability for you to grow for all the right reasons. When you continue to thrive as a business, you will continue to help others and give back. Service helps to shape a positive cycle of support. It can help you to find opportunities, and most importantly of all, to *find purpose.*

From a young age, I began to look for ways to connect with others and have purpose. Service allows me to do both. When I was just a teen, I served on the local community ambulance squad prior to joining the Army. The military was my first foray into a more formal model of service. What I learned during my nearly 20 years in the Army ties into many of the same aspects of service discussed here.

The Army's motto at the time of my enlistment was "Be all that you can be," though it was later replaced by the slogan "An Army of One." While the current slogan is fine, the original promotion was very inspiring to me. It made me see that I could excel beyond my humble beginnings and achieve great things.

Wrestling was equally inspiring and in some ways my participation in it was my first experience with service, because I was serving the good of the team as well as myself. I learned how to control outcomes that benefited not just me but also the success of others on the mat, especially as a good practice partner.

Being of service also goes hand in hand with giving away knowledge about your product and how your business can help others. Informing people draws them to want more information and will help your organization achieve success. Wouldn't you rather work with a company that gives back and is committed to the wellbeing of your community?

With that in mind, one form of service I perform today is donating my time to help non-profit organizations with strategy. Not only do I want to help them to succeed in their missions, but this type of service also often opens further opportunities for business.

As an example, I am an adjunct professor at West Virginia University's School of Medicine, where I lecture young doctors about practice management. I don't get paid, but it is still very beneficial for the students as well as myself.

The lectures help medical residents learn about managing their future practices. It focuses their thoughts, at least for a little while, on the often-overlooked business side of medicine and plants the seed that this may be something they need to become more educated about. Sometimes, these doctors will later contract with our company to help them in this area. Those contracts aren't why I serve as an adjunct professor, but they are a direct result of me being willing to serve others.

Be Of Service

Far beyond what you can gain in your business from being of service, it's simply good for others and good for you. We can learn so much from and through investing our time and talent back into the community both personally and as a local business.

Remember, service benefits you by growing your connections with people who you may not have connected with in any other way. Serving allows you to lead by example and get your team involved in and contributing to the community, as well as fostering a giving culture within your own company.

Takeaways

- What do you do personally to provide service within your community?
- How can you expand your capacity to serve?
- Can you visualize the benefits of service to your team and business as well as to the community and those in need?
- How important is the concept of serving others in your life?

Chapter 8

The Power of Connectivity

Forming connections sounds like simple business, but it's highly rewarding. There's so much power and purpose in connecting resources and people, introducing people, and connecting others to find new opportunities.

Even on social media, I use my brief biographical lines to connect with others, listing myself as a connector, a wrestling coach, and a founder at Forge. I use the word "connector" first, because that is what I am in every aspect of my life. I love connecting people.

Whether in wrestling, in the business community, when I was in the Army, in the various non-profit organizations I'm presently a part of, or in my state, my region, or anywhere in my country – I am always forming connections.

Relationships Drive Success

No matter what you're doing, success and creativity are driven by relationships. One of the main ways I can give back in life is by connecting others to a larger universe of people.

As an example, a few years back I met Mandy Curry. She is extremely passionate about our state and specifically about rural Appalachia. When we first met, she told me that she wanted to give back to the community and help those struggling to get healthy and nutritious foods, such as fresh and locally grown fruit and vegetables. Underserved communities are often food deserts with poor access to healthy food, or the people who live there are unable to afford it. She wanted to provide fresh food that she was growing on her own farm. Her mission was to create abundance where presently there was a lack, so I worked with her on several projects involving connecting food pantries together.

A few years later, when I learned there was a county-owned community kitchen planned for our area, I thought about her. While speaking about the community kitchen project with a local county commissioner, I explained that I knew someone raising fresh fruits and vegetables on her own farm for those who can't access healthy types of food. I suggested the commissioner get in touch with her.

That connection clearly worked. I received a call that the community kitchen was taking off using the fruit and vegetables that Mandy provided. As the years passed, I didn't hear anything more about that partnership until I saw in the local paper that they were being recognized for their good work.

Simply by connecting Mandy and the commissioner, magic happened. Making connections like that is special. It's a kind of connection that benefits so many people. In this case it benefitted those who established the community kitchen, those who worked at it, Mandy and her family, and of course, those folks who needed access to healthy food.

When I connect with people and then simply take a step back and get out of the way, great things can happen. You don't need to stay actively involved once a connection is made, and you don't need to be recognized for making the introduction. The important thing isn't who initiated the connection, just that it was made.

Connection is a powerful tool for establishing businesses as well. Successful businesses like Airbnb and Uber can be attributed to relationships and connecting people. For Airbnb, people have room in a home, and they want other people to occupy it. For Uber, people have cars, and they want to monetize them by using them to transport others. You have a buyer willing to buy and a seller willing to sell. These businesses operate as a force multiplier, a concept that expands depending on how many people engage with it. But it all starts by connecting people together.

What You Give Away Returns to You

To me, the power of connection is limitless. One connection can lead to multiple changes within a community and spread throughout the world.

What you give away comes back to you and multiplies. This is true professionally, in service work, and in personal relationships throughout your life. What we do at Forge is all about connecting our clients with other people and with the right resources. As connectors, we provide what's necessary for our clients to succeed. We show them how to access resources they may not have access to otherwise.

To us, the hero of our success stories is always our client. It's always their story to write; what we do is help them tell it through strategy and connection. Our goal is helping others find new opportunities which brings abundance to them and to our company.

Here's another example. We have a large healthcare community in our area, and as I've mentioned, I've worked with physicians and their families. I'm also an adjunct professor in the School of Medicine for West Virginia

University in the field of practice management. Working with the medical community, I've been able to connect them with resources beyond those of my own business. In doing so, I have created a more valuable relationship for my clients.

By giving away connections and information, I was able to increase our own business by enhancing my relationships with others. I was often able to refer clients or community members to needed medical specialists and to make the phone calls necessary to get an appointment more quickly than the person in need of the referral could on their own.

Nearly 20 years ago, I had a client whose wife needed a cancer specialist. I provided a treatment referral. The specialist had a six month wait, but I was able to circumnavigate that time-period for my client's wife. She was seen in a timely fashion because of my relationship with the physician, and today she's cancer free. My client and his wife were both thankful for the assistance, but honestly, I didn't do anything for the patient. I just made the connection.

That family hasn't forgotten what I did, but for me, it was business as usual. From my standpoint, I am just happy to have these kinds of positive examples that illustrate the importance of relationships and connections.

I'm richly rewarded simply by being part of the solution. When you help good things to occur, that goodness tends to come back to you. My faith leads me to see the purpose of connection and kindness, and of serving others. There is reward enough in doing that work, of being Christ-like, if you will, and hopefully, down the line there's an eternal reward, too.

Building a Strong and Connected Community

When we base our connectivity on a foundation of faith and a sense of purpose, that inherently makes us more capable of resilience through community. Simply having a strong network, regardless of who is in it, creates a sense of belonging that provides emotional support when facing both personal and professional challenges.

Connectivity also provides access to diverse perspectives and enables you to engage with a wide range of people, viewpoints, and ideas — all of which can enhance your creativity and expand your ability to problem-solve effectively.

<u>Takeaways</u>

- Do you have people in your life who you have considered connecting? Have you done so?
- Do you believe that relationships connect people and drive business?
- Can you think of ways you can connect people in your life or business?

Chapter 9

Know Your Value

"Never doubt that a small group of thoughtful, committed, citizens can change the world. Indeed, it is the only thing that ever has."

Margaret Mead

    Connectivity and service are both ways to personally realize your own value. But beyond encouraging team members to join you in service and showing them the power of connectivity, how do you let the members of your team know that they're valuable?

    One way to express their value to you is to include your team and their perspectives when making a large decision. At

Forge, as CEO, I get to make the final call; I'm responsible for that.

But getting the perspective of others is still vital to achieving success. By seeking opinions from my team, I'm showing them that I value their knowledge. Including their thoughts and ideas is also valuable for achieving success with any plan, as someone may have an insightful viewpoint you hadn't previously considered.

Be inclusive throughout your organization. If you consider just one person's position, success may be limited. But if you consider everyone's input, you are more likely to make successful decisions that are best for the organization.

Your goal should be to know and understand your teammates and their strengths as well as knowing your own. Know where you fit into a team.

Knowing Your Value and Fit

It's important to know you're valued in an organization yourself, just as it's important to value others. Before anyone can fully understand and appreciate others' value, they must first know how to recognize those qualities in themselves.

Honestly assess and consider where your own value is the strongest. By doing so, you'll uncover the best places for you to contribute to your team. Understanding each person's value, including your own, is important for both your satisfaction and for organizational satisfaction.

Focusing your efforts on the tasks where you can provide the most value will help your organization to achieve its ultimate potential as you achieve your own. Express and leverage your value into your efforts and work.

I was struck by a line in the film *Gettysburg*, which was written and directed by Ronald F. Maxwell. In the film, the Union's Colonel Chamberlain receives Confederate prisoners of war. He's told he can do anything he wants to them, even kill them, but instead, he turns to them and says that he values them. Every person has value. His character does this because ultimately, he wants them to remember that they are all Americans, and they will all be part of the same union again someday.

I think quite a bit about that line and the idea that every person has value, regardless of their position. As a leader, remember your own value and acknowledge that every person in your organization has their own value they can contribute to the team. Then do what you can to encourage their efforts by giving proper acknowledgement when team members succeed. Remember, *what gets rewarded gets repeated*.

Acknowledge the Strength in Our Differences

One part of acknowledging value is shaping a creative environment where team members can best articulate their own value, where they can be proactive and innovative. Remember what we covered earlier about the importance of motivational alignment: finding the right role for each person's skillset makes them more positive and productive. No strategy is more effective at creating a productive atmosphere than shaping the workplace environment, and this is just one more method for doing so.

As a leader, establish an organizational environment in which each team member is valued and appreciated. Provide the team with opportunities to shape and express their value to the group. Most importantly, acknowledge the strength in differences. You can elevate the strength of your organization and bring your team together to achieve even more of their, and your, goals by recognizing and utilizing the important differences in your team members' skills and approaches.

Establishing a Team Approach

Establishing a team within your organization instead of a culture of employer/employee means that you can operate as partners in a winning strategy. Where an employee may be thought of as replaceable or re-assignable, a team member is most valuable in the position in which they are most skilled. That's a win for both your team members and for your organization.

Think of it this way. If you're coaching a baseball team, you can't have a team member working as the first and third baseman at the same time. They would never succeed in either role. If that team member is more successful and valuable as the first baseman, then that's where they should be.

It's the same in business. Place your team members in positions where they can perform successfully. Embrace their differences to make sure they are in exactly the right role to be successful.

Doing so enhances not just their own performance but that of the entire team. We are stronger together, working as a team. If we understand and are celebrated for our own unique contributions and we are placed into the positions where we bring the most value, we are each stronger individually. And, as is essential for your organization, the team is collectively stronger, too.

Stay Agile

Embracing your team's value also depends on your own agility and that of your team members. Returning to the baseball analogy, there may be a time when you need your first baseman to stand in on third base. It's the same in business. Encourage your team members to embrace agility. At times there may need to be some movement, an exchange of positions, or a new form of action that your team members will need to embrace. After all, situations and required work do change. It's vital to be flexible and move people based on the dynamics of any given situation. You may even need to take some team members out of rotation for an inning, or bench them, as necessary.

Adaptability is another area where it's important to accentuate positive achievements and the value of your teammates. Cross train them when you can, giving them the opportunity to learn new areas of the company. Doing so may open new doors for them and for your company. If you give someone who has had success at one aspect of running a project the chance to become a project manager, you may be mentoring someone who shows a great capacity for learning and growth. By doing these kinds of shifts in the positions of your team, you can cause other dynamics to shift, setting the stage for greater organizational achievement.

Team Dynamics

The dynamic of your team sets your organization up for success. Everyone should be rowing the boat in the same direction, not fighting each other's oars. Everyone must work together to reach the finish line. It's the same in any organization. Working together is the way to achieve success on a specific project or for the business to thrive in general terms.

Successful team dynamics must include:

- Communicating between team members and the team leader
- Evaluating team member achievements
- Recognizing achievements
- Learning skills
- Understanding organizational purpose and vision
- Encouraging and facilitating improvement

The evaluation should focus on improving the dynamics of the team, including improving your ability to move the positions of team members if necessary to shift dynamics for greater success.

Dynamics can be affected internally, like an individual's ability to in their current role. They can also be affected by external factors such as the economy, customer needs and demands, or necessary shifts due to unexpected events such as a pandemic. There may be personal external shifts as well, based on family life and health matters. Regardless of the reason, paying attention to and adjusting team dynamics is another integral part of running a successful organization.

Every cog must fit in the place where it is the most useful and the most productive. It must be connected to other parts for the overall organization to work well. Similarly, within an organization every team member must work and connect, even if they are working on different projects or different aspects of an organization's operations. Leadership starts with making sure that your team is working effectively together as a part of a whole.

Picking Up the Slack

In a successful organization, everyone knows and appreciates the value they offer and the value that others bring to the group. Another aspect is the ability of team members to pick up the slack for another when necessary. Dividing and sharing responsibilities when called upon to do so is essential when life challenges or work challenges occur.

As a personal example, I was getting my MBA over the course of five semesters. My wife and I were both working, and my wife was also pregnant with our first child. With so much going on personally, I was not 100% on top of things all the time in my MBA classes.

In those classes we were broken into small teams. When my wife was having our son and I had extensive responsibilities at home, the others in my team picked up my slack. When things got a little calmer at home, I was able to step up to fill the gaps for other teammates when they were experiencing challenges or life changes.

Being able to step in when needed is essential. By knowing the dynamics of your team and what may be affecting any given team member, you can fill in or have others fill in, when necessary, to keep all the cogs turning. You can still run a successful team even when one team member needs to step back a bit from taking their turn at bat.

Mindfulness author and speaker Brene Brown created a video about marriage, the gist of which is also eminently relatable to the idea of teams. She said that no one is ever evenly contributing 50% in a 50/50 shared relationship. Contributions will fluctuate based on situations. Similarly, you often hear the common idiom that everyone should "Give 100%." That idea is equally absurd. No one can give 100% all the time. There are always other circumstances outside of any given situation or organization.

Everyone operates on different levels depending on the day and what other aspects of their lives impact their work. When other team members are there to help pick up the slack, you can achieve the highest value throughout your organization.

In my experience on wrestling teams, champions are made in pairs: you and your workout partner. For success, you both must put in the work, be dedicated, and be willing to challenge and push each other to that next level.

Think of your team members in any organization as your partners. The military operates similarly. You are encouraged to accomplish your mission. But the team you're a part of does not give up on you even if you give up on yourself. When you know that others have your back, that they haven't given up on you, that's what's needed to push forward, move through any difficult periods, and not give up after all. No one is left behind.

Competition and Rewards

When it comes to team dynamics and enhancing performances, internally, rewarding achievement is the best leadership tool. However, both competition and reward can be helpful in shaping success.

When I say competition, I don't mean creating internal competitions between team members. That type of situation can create resentment or shape relationships that are more challenging and may have unintended consequences. Even friendly competitions can be bad for long-term team dynamics. Certainly, if you have two team members who both hear, understand, and believe that their partner or teammate is terrific, that acknowledgement can encourage both to keep doing great work, to keep up with or even outdo each other while still supporting each other, with the company as the ultimate winner. But even a positive race for achievement can end up causing resentment that negatively impacts the whole team.

Overall, I think it is far more important and effective to recognize and reward team members, so that they will repeat their own winning behavior. It can be a slippery slope to compare one employee's performance versus another's.

Recognition and reward will always trump competition within the organization. Viewing your organization's team members as all communicating, all rowing in the same direction, is far more important than encouraging internal competition for an organization's ultimate success.

Often, just as I tell our wrestlers, you are your biggest competitor. You are wrestling against yourself to achieve your personal best. Self-improvement will always be a more effect motivator than striving to be better than someone you should be working with, not against.

Since it doesn't destabilize the group, there are some cases where external competition with other organizations can be motivating. Working to achieve more than a competitor in the same field may be the push your team needs to secure a new contract or continue an existing business relationship. Just ensure that any competition doesn't overpower self-driven desire to succeed. In the end, your team must work together in a positive environment – one that you establish.

Takeaways

- Have you ever picked up the slack for other organization team members or in personal relationships?
    - Do you feel others have picked up the slack for you? Why or why not?
- Have you let your team know they are valued? How have you done so?
- Do you believe that rewarding team members leads to repeated success?
    - Can you cite instances when this has occurred? Why or why not?

Chapter 10

Stakeholder Importance

Identifying the stakeholders for any project your company is working on is just as important as creating a team and working together. Both are key for developing and deploying your organizational strategy.

For any organization, a successful project includes these areas:

- Gather information and ideas
- Obtain feedback and buy-ins
- Establish accepted critical strategy and performance goals

When creating an organizational strategic plan, it's essential for you to include the team members who are striving to achieve common goals for your organization.

After working with your team to include them on the purpose of the project, initiating the process of any new endeavor should start with interviewing the stakeholders who are involved.

What gets said at these interviews is the important thing – not who said what.

Sometimes members of leadership do not attend these meetings to make sure that team members feel they can speak freely.

In developing any successful organizational strategy, stakeholder meetings are critical throughout each phase of the planning process.

- Discover
- Explore
- Build
- Deploy

During this Explore phase, it's important to include all the stakeholders involved with overall strategy or a specific piece of the strategic plan.

Benefits of Stakeholder Inclusion

One major benefit of getting stakeholder input during the Explore phase is that this process allows them to provide their ideas. It doesn't mean doing all the things they suggest, but it does mean considering their perspective. Additionally, it may provide an alternative way of conceiving your action plan for their benefit.

Speaking of benefits – you'll benefit enormously from receiving that all-important buy-in from participants. Making stakeholders feel as if they are a part of your mission makes them more likely to support the plan and help carry it out, rather than feeling left out and disengaged because they were not considered.

Stepping Back from Stakeholder Meetings

Since our company operates as a trusted advisor, it is important that our client is secure enough for senior leadership to step back and allow the stakeholders to interact comfortably with other members of our team. This speaks to their comfort level with the team. It also allows stakeholders to give a more honest opinion and be clear about any concerns and ideas.

Allowing anonymous contributions encourages those who might have remained silent to speak up. After all, *the main goal is to get good data from stakeholder meetings,* not to intimidate them into agreement with a plan. They should be willing to share freely without worrying about being reprimanded or discounted. Trust me, I have worked in environments where this is the case, and you won't get honest feedback or ideas this way.

Utilizing a Strong Facilitator

If senior leadership is not present in a stakeholder meeting, it is even more important to choose a strong facilitator. The last thing that you want is for someone to sour a group dynamic by turning a stakeholder meeting into a complaint session.

Sometimes participants are already willing to share, while others need a push. To encourage sharing, you need to have someone present from your team who can acknowledge their position and be capable of moving from individual to individual or from subject to subject in the meeting.

The goal is always to gain stakeholder trust. Remember, the important thing is what is being said, not who said it or why. We try to protect anonymity in summaries and reports of stakeholder meetings rather than directly quoting anyone to the client. You're really seeking to identify and manage risks. Stakeholder engagement allows proactive management and mitigation strategies.

I am always upfront about telling the business owners and leaders we work with that this is how we operate. You want to be transparent about the process and make sure they are comfortable with it. If they are not, then we do not have to proceed that way.

Several years ago, I conducted an anonymous employee opinion survey for a company. We collected surveys that were not numbered or otherwise identifiable and presented them to company leadership. There were some comments that caused that leadership to express a need to find out who said a certain thing, so that they could help them find a different opportunity outside that organization, if you know what I mean. I let them know that I couldn't ethically do that; I had given my word that the surveys were anonymous. The whole idea of a stakeholder group is getting the best possible data set, not "outing" someone who is dissatisfied or doesn't agree with an initial plan.

Of course, some leaders find diversity of thought threatening. But having healthy debates and a variety of thinking can help to determine a plan of action and assist with accomplishing a successful buy-in for a plan. We don't have to agree with each other 100% of the time, but we should be able to respect different thinking. We will never know what people are thinking and they will not be able to express their thoughts if we don't allow them the space to safely express themselves.

Every stakeholder's opinion is valuable to hear, and more so collectively than individually. Sometimes the CFO is going to tell you that you can't spend any money. The Human Resources leader will tell you that you can't change anyone's position or let someone go. Everyone will have a different opinion. That is okay. If you try and do what everyone tells you, you may not accomplish anything. However, if you listen to all opinions collectively, then you can shape the best possible decision for the group.

The Pearl Necklace Analogy

Each person in an organization is like an individual pearl in his or her own right. But until you string those pearls together, you don't realize the full value. The value is in the necklace and all the pearls fitting together cohesively to create a more beautiful and valuable whole.

That cohesiveness is what brings us together. We look for individual feedback and express the importance of each stakeholder with the goal of bringing each pearl together to shape a necklace – a beautiful decision that's good for everyone.

That's what creates a successful team culture in both our organization as well as a client's company. Everyone expresses their differing thoughts and opinions, and at the end of the day, everyone is part of the same team.

This leads to:

- Improved project outcomes
- Involvement of stakeholders in project planning and execution
- A stronger culture
- Assurance that diverse needs and expectations are considered and addressed

Take everyone's feedback and make the best decision based on the data you've gathered. That's what stakeholder inclusion is all about, and that is how you make, shape, and instigate a successful project, both internally and externally.

Takeaways

- Who are your stakeholders?
- Have you engaged stakeholders with a project prior to commencing its implementation?
- Do you feel getting the opinions of others is key to the successful buy in on a project?
    - Are you able to step back and let others facilitate a meeting for anonymity when appropriate?
- How do you implement stakeholder engagement?

Chapter 11

Engage the Critic

He has the right to criticize who has the heart to help."

Abraham Lincoln

Getting input and buy-in from your critics is what I like to call the "secret sauce" of successful strategic planning. It's your hidden weapon for building a team and negotiating consensus among team members or stakeholders.

Stick to an agenda and let others serve as constructive critics. By truly engaging them you'll be in a far better position for planning than by assuming silence is consent and leaving them out. After all, when critics are included rather than excluded, they will be considerably more likely to support a plan of action and feel tied to its success.

Make People a Part of the Plans That Impact Them

Optimally, we want people – stakeholders, or any individual involved in planning – to be a part of those plans and invested in their outcome.

As noted, at Forge, we work to create stakeholder engagement as a key aspect of the strategic planning process. We start by identifying stakeholders in the plan, and making certain that the planning will be inclusive, inviting, and seeking input from all pertinent stakeholders. Even if they do not participate actively, simply by inviting them to do so, the stakeholders will typically be more likely to support the plan and have an investment in its success.

The Mistake of Excluding the Critic

If a stakeholder feels left out of the process, they will be less likely to support the plan. A person perceived as a critic or as a more negative, "glass-half-empty" type of individual will often be excluded from the process because of their reputation.

But even if a person is seemingly known to be a malcontent, the critic is still the person that I want to bring into the planning process. For me, it is a mistake to exclude them.

For one thing, the critic will usually be the first to suggest any shortcomings or gaps in a plan – after all, being a critic is their forte. Expressing their concerns can expose flaws that might otherwise be missed during the planning process. Their involvement may also disrupt "groupthink" solutions where everyone nods along to a poorly thought-out plan. Both options make it easier to avoid pitfalls when executing on the plan.

At the very least, by including the critic in the planning process, they will feel involved in it, and perhaps even invested in it. This removes any potential for a victim mentality to develop and potentially heads off future problems.

Look at the big picture when including the critic in planning. By bringing them into your discussions, you will be heading off the kinds of situations where critics are most comfortable, complaining in private to a small group that can be vocal enough to derail any plan down the line. I call this "watercooler talk."

Increasing Your Planning Awareness

Along with promoting the inclusivity of the critic, you'll likely find that you're increasing your awareness during planning. Remember, it's the critic who may show you something you missed during the planning process.

In a professional context, engaging with critics can lead to improvements in products, services, and quality. You are providing critics with the opportunity to address any shortcomings in the planning and to enhance the overall performance of a strategy.

With all this in mind, the critic is the exact person I want to pull into any conversation. They will sharpen my own problem-solving skills and address any gaps in planning. They will point out any flaws or shortcomings because that is what they are best at doing. As a result, the plan will end up being stronger from hearing them voice their concerns or disagreements.

Critics may point out that money could be best spent on more essential or different things than you've considered. For example, they might point out that funds are being directed at more visible, public-facing projects such as a new entrance marquee rather than being used behind the scenes for unseen but necessary vehicle maintenance.

Similarly, they may point out valuable information that you were unaware of that could change the direction of your planning For example, you may only know that a new marketing plan is necessary for a company and not have the background information that the company is working with outdated computers unable to implement the new marketing plans. Providing information like this is invaluable, because now you'll know that technology will need to be replaced before starting the new program.

These are the kind of criticisms that can cause a valuable addition or change to strategic planning, whether that ends up being investing in new infrastructure or choosing a more vital but previously unconsidered area of the company's operations to address.

In the book *Team of Rivals*, author Doris Kearns Goodwin relates that then newly elected President Abraham Lincoln appointed his political foes to his cabinet, welcoming them on his team saying that he believed they were better and more knowledgeable on certain subjects than he was. Including those individuals on his team made him more successful in office because they presented information and criticism that he wouldn't have access to otherwise.

Motivating the Critic

Along with the kinds of valuable information that a critic can provide, involving them in the planning process is also a motivational tool. Not only will it bring them more fully on board with the process, but it will also provide some empowerment by giving them the opportunity to engage.

I once worked on a contract for a federal agency. One entity within the cohort of stakeholders was a unionized group that I needed to work with. Union leadership members were expected to be critical, as they did not have a good relationship with management at the laboratory as they felt unheard and disregarded.

Once I started to engage with them weekly, they began to add valuable ideas and input. By acknowledging that their ideas were important, they were able to buy into the planning process and eventually develop a more constructive relationship with management and others in the laboratory.

Relationships are crucial in every aspect of business and life. As I've said before, what you're rewarded for doing is what becomes repeated behavior. By rewarding these union members with active listening and engagement, and by advocating for them, I became the man to see when there were problems. I was able to forge a new kind of relationship with them. They began to express their opinions and concerns and offer their valuable input to me because they knew they would be heard.

Improve Communication and Persuasion Skills

Responding to critics also requires clear, effective communication which can hone your ability to articulate and defend your positions persuasively.

You'll need to be sure that the critic fully understands what you're communicating, because in many cases they'll only hear what they want or expect to hear.

Because you'll be forced to work on being the best communicator you can be, you'll improve your ability to clearly articulate your plan and your vision. Convince the critic to be on board and to feel that they are a valued part of the process. Making sure that you are being understood and that they are being valued will help you improve your levels of persuasion and show you new ways to incentivize and engage. It will even elevate your resourcefulness and leadership skills.

It's not about walking on eggshells around the critic. Rather, it is about engaging clearly and carefully, which is particularly important if the critic may also be an influencer within the organization.

If you make promises, fulfill them. When commitments are made, be sure you keep them. If you don't, trust will be lost, and your integrity will be weakened. If mistakes are made along the way, own them so the critic has no reason to share and criticize any errors and turn others against you.

Overall, you must communicate. You must be clear, concise, and articulate, and be sure that your actions support what you say with integrity.

Avoiding Overly Engaging the Critic

The critic is always going to be present. As noted, in many cases their presence will help you make your process better and will make you sharper. But for all the good a critic can bring to a project, too much criticism can also be detrimental.

Boundaries need to be established with critics. You can't constantly reward the critic who sends the wrong message to others on your team who are more positive.

Be able to acknowledge that you've heard or received their input, considered it, and now it is time to move forward with your mission. Recognize that there is a line between being appropriately critical and inappropriately obstinate.

If the critic is being critical of a concept, process or business approach, that is acceptable. But don't allow criticism about personal matters or others on the team to emerge.

A good leader must define boundaries and consistently enforce them. If boundaries are crossed, ask the critic to rephrase their criticism or let them know that you do not have time for that type of discussion. When you respond in this way once or twice, you'll have made a successful course correction. The critic will usually be reluctant to voice these kinds of comments again.

Be careful about the type of culture and environment that you're creating. Don't feed negative culture by listening to critics speaking about *people* instead of *process.*

Don't engage the critic just to let them walk all over you. Set up boundaries as appropriate and be careful of the culture that you create. But remember the value of including critics in your process.

Takeaways

- Do you actively include the "critic" in your strategic planning? Why or why not?
- Are you able to set up appropriate boundaries while still inviting the critic into your core group?
- Have you used clear and effective communication techniques when responding to critics? Can you describe what those skills mean to you?

Chapter 12

Blueprint Your Way

Along with engaging stakeholders and including critics, establishing a blueprint is critical to reach your goals. No matter what you're doing in life, you need to construct a plan. The blueprint serves as a foundation for organizational strategy, one that identifies your goals, objectives, and key results. It provides a clear direction which helps in aligning your efforts and resources towards success with your mission, vision, objectives, and key results.

From Starting Point to Destination

We use blueprints in so many aspects of our lives, whether we are building a house, going on a vacation, or using GPS to find the fastest, most economical route from where you are now to where you want to be. A blueprint is just as necessary in business.

Both starting point and destination are crucial. The starting point allows you to understand your current place or state. Know where you stand right now, today: your strengths, your weaknesses, your value, the areas which need improvement. Know who you are and who you are not.

That can be a challenge for small businesses. It can be difficult not to be everything to everyone yet trying to do so dilutes your value and who you are. Having a blueprint will help illuminate the path forward.

Once you know your current state, decide where you want to end up. Identify your mission and vision. What will make your mission successful? That's your true destination: defining what success looks like.

Building Strategy

Your blueprint is the foundation on which you build your strategy to move forward.

We offer our clients at Forge a blueprint service, through which we identify the vision and the mission of the organization and the objective of the plan that we're constructing. We help craft an organization's strategic plan or a business development plan. We look at the main pillars or focus areas of the client's objectives and define key results. That becomes the blueprint, or the foundation for strategy.

Having a blueprint for your business is essentially like having a blueprint for building a home. No one would want to invest in a business or a house that has no plan. Make sure the house is level, plumb, and square. Make sure the roof fits correctly. Measure twice and cut once. Blueprints let you see exactly what your house will look like – only then can you build it to spec. Define what your success will look like and build your business in the same way.

Measure What Matters

Once you've defined what success looks like, measure your progress toward that success. Focus on important metrics that are worth tracking.

Your budget is one area that is key to measure, whether you are running a business or a nonprofit organization. Measure expenses, profit, margin, and revenue. You'll also want to measure employee satisfaction, growth, and performance.

Of course, that's only one parameter. The milestones that are most important will vary depending on the project. When you know what success looks like to you, identify the milestones along that path. It's also important to know what success does *not* look like, and to have that clarity of vision.

As it says in Proverbs 29,

> *"Where there is no vision, the people perish."*

Your blueprint provides the vision you need from a strategic planning perspective.

Identify your vision first and be sure that your mission aligns with it. If it doesn't, either your mission or vision needs work.

Company Vision, Goals, Objectives, and Results

Defining your company's vision, goals, objectives, and desired results begins with your blueprint.

Your blueprint should always include:

- Your company's vision and its future. This is what you strive for, your aspiration.
- Your mission. Your mission is a tangible accomplishment, and you can have more than one mission. Missions are more easily measured than vision.

- Your goals. To achieve your mission, you need to identify your goals and objectives – your objectives are the key results that you want to achieve.
- Your key results. These are what allow you to measure practical things such as return on investment. Developing your objectives and key results will show you what success looks like. Success shows you your return on investment.

When we work with an organization on a strategic plan, we look at their overall objective. What are they trying to achieve? We examine the key results they're seeking and whether those results are to increase profitability, create efficiency, lower expenses, or reduce turnover.

Measuring data is helpful, but what do you want to do with it? Consider the outcome you want to accomplish. At Forge, once we can determine the objective and the key results you're looking for, then the data becomes useful in defining objectives and key results.

Data always needs to be connected to efforts, actions, and results. Effort only goes so far and doesn't always lead to desired results, especially without a solid plan.

Success Management

With the blueprint in place, refer to it as needed to ensure you are progressing in the right direction. Once we've completed a strategic plan, we focus on success management. A success management plan allows us to work with our clients to manage the ongoing success of their strategy. It needs to be an agile plan that can evolve as necessary.

While your vision should rarely if ever change, missions can be a little more agile. They may change as necessary, although not constantly. From there, moving down to your goals, objectives, results, and strategies, it's important to be able to course correct, and be sure your vision, mission, and results are in alignment.

We offer a traceability matrix for our clients that allows us to track progress using metrics. With this tool, we can be sure that our clients are achieving success by using the plan we developed. We can course correct and modify as necessary.

Creating a Clear Direction

Creating a blueprint provides the direction to build an organizational strategic pace, identifying key areas and objectives to determine a clear path for the organization's leaders to build upon.

By following that blueprint's direction, our clients can achieve and build an effective strategic plan.

Focused and Improved Decision Making

A blueprint also helps organizations avoid distractions and focus on vision, objectives, and key results.

It's an objective approach, one that precludes members of the organization from taking a planning conversation in the direction that most benefits them personally rather than the organization as a whole.

Having a blueprint lets you choose and prioritize:

- Strategies
- Objectives
- Tactics that help you achieve them

Regardless of the type of plan we are building, the blueprint reveals priorities, level of effort gaps, a company's current and future state, and where you are today versus where you want to be. The blueprint can be used at many different levels throughout an organization.

Shaping a Personal Blueprint

Having a blueprint is important not just in business, but in your personal life as well. Having a solid idea of where you want to go with your life, your personal goals, and what you enjoy – plus taking stock of your blessings - is key to your happiness and personal growth opportunities.

We certainly have blueprint plans in place for our three children, because we want to give them every opportunity and plan for their future. A blueprint also assists with areas of finance such as the household budget, how we spend money, the best use of our resources, and plans for retirement.

We have plans for our personal health, including diet and exercise, that we work toward achieving. As you move through life, I encourage people to be selective about their time, and to go where they are valued. That is part of having a successful blueprint, too.

Go where you are celebrated, not just tolerated. Spend your time with those who appreciate you and recognize your value. Even though it is easier said than done, say no when you want to, and encourage others to step in.

A Blueprint Is Critical in Reaching Goals

When you use mapping software, an app such as Waze can't build a path from your starting point to your destination without knowing where you want to go. Creating a blueprint works in the same way. Build your path forward from the place you are now before you begin to follow just any route. Measure the direction and the distance.

Along the way, ask yourself repeatedly if your thoughts, actions, and outcomes align with your vision and mission. The clear direction and focus provided by the blueprint should allow you to simplify decisions. Ask yourself if whatever you're thinking about doing is contributing to achieving your vision. If the answer is yes, then whatever you are doing is good for your strategic plan. If the answer is no, it's best to drop what you are doing and move on. This will ensure that your choices are made in alignment with your overall objectives for easier execution and measurement.

Remember, your blueprint is a tool you can keep returning to over time. It can assist with filtering new ideas and strategies that look tempting at the time, but which don't lead to the success of your mission.

Takeaways

- Do you have a personal blueprint for your life? If so, how do you employ it?
- How can you use the blueprint as a tool and reference for keeping your focus on vision, mission, and objectives with key results?

- Have you found it to be true that effort does not always lead to results?
- What are your initiatives, actions, and outcomes – and how do they align with your vision and mission?

Chapter 13

Process Is Critical

"Never tell people how to do things. Tell them what to do and they will surprise you with their ingenuity."

General George S. Patton

    Like having a blueprint, a process-oriented approach is important in all aspects of our lives but is especially crucial in business. Whenever we apply process development or improvement, we are examining both how to accomplish a process or series of processes and how to continue them. It's essential to have processes in place to shape a successful strategic plan of any kind, both personally and professionally.

Document Your Process

Even though processes are crucial, companies with less than 100 employees typically don't document theirs. This becomes an especially critical problem if potential acquirers want to understand your work and decide whether your business is worth acquiring in the first place.

We work with many businesses that are excellent at what they do, from manufacturers to glass makers. Many are family businesses, and when the owner wants to sell their company, if their processes aren't documented, the value and price of the business drops considerably to perspective buyers.

The processes used to create strategic plans for any organization are not just key for its success in the present but for its value in the future. Whether your process is how to perform surgery or build a bridge, having a process-oriented approach is crucial.

At Forge, we have a method that identifies:

- What triggers a process
- What are the key inputs for that process
- The output of the process being deployed

There are many great process methods available to follow, so choose one that fits your business model. Once you have a process in place, it will allow your business to operate concisely while also driving up the value and equity of your company.

As an example, we have a small family business client which is run successfully by a husband-and-wife team. They purchased a 30-year-old company originally owned by another family. When the original owner passed away, most of the existing processes were undocumented. Fortunately, the new owners were able to work with others who knew the company and were able to recreate those processes. But so many other businesses put into that position are not as fortunate to be able to do so and close.

When processes are not documented this can negatively impact the sale of businesses and generational wealth. In rural Appalachia, it's not uncommon to come across a small business such as a hardware store that has been operating for 100 years. The owner's descendants have moved on to become doctors or lawyers, or successful business owners in another field.

These individuals are unlikely to be interested in running that hardware store, so instead of selling a still-productive business, they have a fire sale, selling off all the equipment, stock, and any real estate before closing the store. This has a negative effect not just on generational wealth for the future, but also on the community, which now has a shuttered store and must go elsewhere to purchase hardware supplies, incurring increased costs while reducing the business tax base. Without documented processes, both a business and the community where it's located stand to lose a great deal.

Documenting Process

Depending on what our clients' needs are, we will discuss whether they have documented their policies, procedures, and processes. We implement this documentation as part of their strategic plan. This can be particularly vital for new entrepreneurs who may not have considered documentation at all.

I encourage stakeholders to begin thinking about selling their business on the day that they start it. Building your business around selling it is key to your present and future success. If that is not something that is part of your overall business plan, why not? It certainly should be.

If your business does not document its process, the business does not sell, it closes.

Is Your Business Sellable?

One of the questions we ask business owners from the first moment we begin to work with them is this: "Would you buy your business?"

As president of the Country Roads Angel Network, the first accredited angel investing network in the state of West Virginia, we support and encourage start-ups. We see so many small businesses that could be bought by entrepreneurs, and thus have a viable business with which they could be making money from day one. However, if that business has no processes in place, such a sale becomes much less likely.

Connecting and encouraging business entrepreneurs who want to sell with those who want to buy is something that I enjoy. It's also something that could have a large, positive economic impact across the whole country collectively. But again, a process must be in place to run the business being sold.

Documenting your sales process within a business is especially vital. In many small businesses, it's all about making a sale. No one thinks to document the *process* of *making* that sale, which is potentially a great deal more valuable than the individual sale itself. Maximize that value through documentation. Document your sales process which is going to be unique for your business – not unique to the one person who is making the sale. This will help when hiring a new sales associate and when selling your business.

Additionally, by documenting your process, you can evaluate its efficiency and make notes about process benchmarks. You can change or tweak your process to make it more successful. When a new entrepreneur comes in to purchase your business, you can show them your inventory, your accounts receivable, your customer base, and your processes both in terms of sales and marketing, as well as your technical processes.

We use a four-step development process to approach every aspect of our work. I've presented it before when reviewing and supporting your team members and your clients' needs, but it's an excellent one to apply to any business:

Discover: We discover what our client needs, get to know what they do, research, and better understand their market, opportunities, challenges, barriers to entry, each of these areas.

Explore: Once we discover and understand our client's work, we deliver what we call an explorer report, including an industry analysis and market analysis and a feasibility study as part of the tools and resources needed to build a plan for that client.

FORGE PROCESS

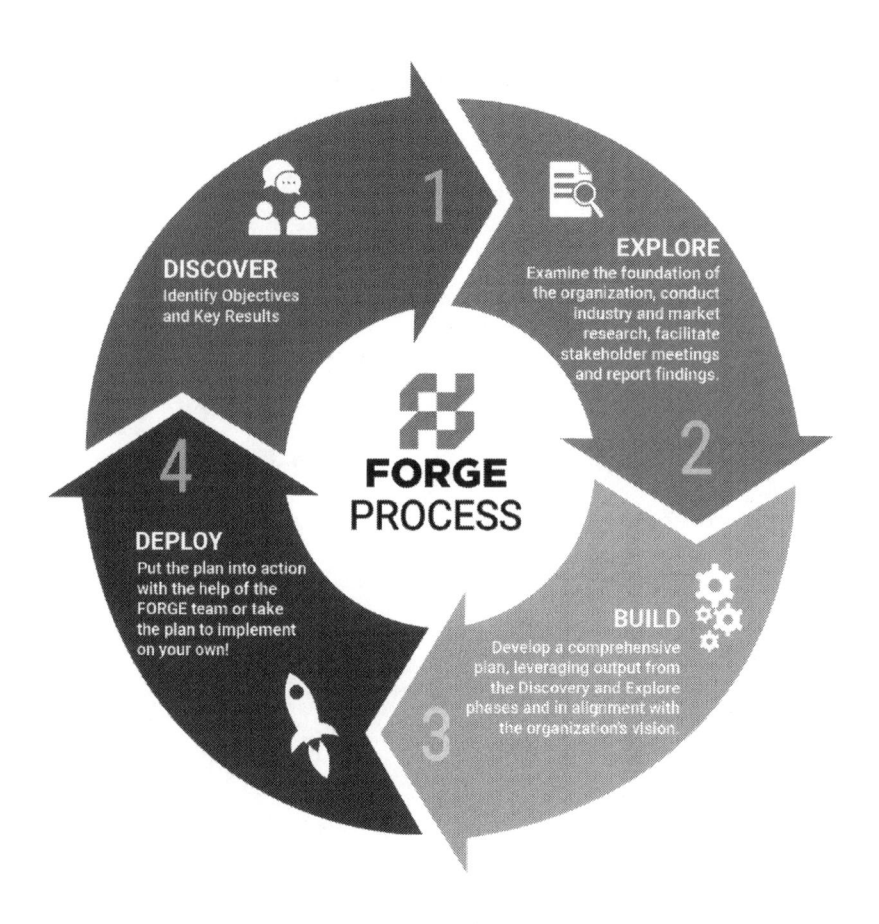

1. DISCOVER — Identify Objectives and Key Results

2. EXPLORE — Examine the foundation of the organization, conduct industry and market research, facilitate stakeholder meetings and report findings.

3. BUILD — Develop a comprehensive plan, leveraging output from the Discovery and Explore phases and in alignment with the organization's vision.

4. DEPLOY — Put the plan into action with the help of the FORGE team or take the plan to implement on your own!

Build: Armed with the information and feedback from our client, we move into the plan building stage. We create a blueprint and plan; we follow that process.

Deploy: With a blueprint and strategic plan complete, the execution can begin.

We use this four-step process in everything we do, from training programs to strategic or business development and execution plans.

As Stephen Covey famously wrote,

> *"Seek first to understand, then to be understood."*

That's what establishing and following processes – and documenting them – is all about.

Improved Problem Solving

A process-oriented approach to your business can lead to more effective problem-solving and continuous improvement for your company.

Establishing the right processes for you will help you think in terms of what problem or problems you may be encountering, what the solution may be for your problems, and what you expect will happen after you implement that solution or solutions.

The place to start is always by identifying first what it is that's triggering your need for a solution. Then ask yourself what materials or actions you need to put into place to implement your solution. What will your input be to implement that solution? Then get to work. Finally, once the process has been activated, look at what the output or outcome of that process has been.

Take a look at what happened after you implemented your planned solution. Did you get what you needed from the solution? If not, you'll need to reconfigure your solution to better address the triggers and issues that precipitated the need for the process in the first place.

Remember, if you start building a solution before you know what your needs really are, chances are that you'll have to go back and rebuild a different solution. This is inefficient, stressful, and ineffective. Instead, reduce stress and inefficiency by using techniques that provide established, repeatable ways to solve problems. Using these techniques reduces the enormous cognitive load of continual decision-making and planning.

By going beyond what is required of you in any given moment and performing an analysis of circumstances in a process-oriented manner, your business will become less stressful, more successful, and ultimately more sellable.

Takeaways

- Are you documenting the processes that make your business run consistently?

- Have you adopted any procedures for creating the processes for your business to follow? Why or why not?
- Are you thinking of your business as a sellable venture that in the years ahead can be turnkey for a buyer?

Chapter 14

Give It Away

What does it mean to "give it away?" Most business owners would agree that if you "give it away" you won't be in business very long. But giving away knowledge and information can be viewed as an investment. It is an investment in your current clients, your future customers, or your community.

For myself personally and at Forge, we have a unique sales approach about giving away plentifully. Give away education, give away information – give away enough that the people who receive benefits from these giveaways may eventually become our clients.

This book represents an example of that "give it away" philosophy and approach. I want to be helpful to you and your business and provide the insight that you can use to be successful. My hope is that you'll find value within these pages for your business and your life.

Giving knowledge away is one of my purposes in life, and I hope that by sharing my knowledge with you, you'll carry that tradition forward.

Knowledge is Power

I'm sure you've heard it said that knowledge is power. We give information, knowledge, and power away. Why?

First, it gets people thinking, and plants the seed of growth. You need to plant a seed to get growth in return.

While I don't have to give away every detail, I am a big believer in giving away some good advice, information, and even some solutions. Up to a certain level, I enjoy sharing the knowledge I have and sharing my ability to empower others. Giving knowledge helps others to think about their needs and how to implement solutions that could change things in their businesses or their lives for the better.

Some people will start to think about their needs and then decide they could do some strategic planning on their own. My response is that this may very well be true, but it may not be the most beneficial thing to do. You could also cut your own hair, but if you are not a trained hair stylist, is that a good idea?

I'm simply not afraid of losing business because I am giving away good information. For me, over the last 20 years, the opposite has occurred most often.

At one point early in my career I was working as the head of private banking for a start-up bank. When the bank first began, the CEO and I met with the deans of local university's dental and medical schools to discuss a possible collaboration. The bank offered financing and home lending to medical doctors. To reach the doctors in the dental and medical programs, we came up with an idea to teach a class on finance and how to get a mortgage. We decided that we would not solicit or even mention our bank, which would not be in line with the school program rules.

With all of this in mind, we began to teach a course in which the residents and future doctors and dentists would learn about personal finance, investment types and options, mortgage lending, and the basics of contract law. These were all important real-life lessons which these students typically do not receive in medical or dental schools. However, the institutions cared enough about their students to want them to be financially stable.

Over 20 years of administering these education programs, I've never taken a single dollar to do so. Today, even though I am no longer in banking, I continue to teach these programs. Many of the resident physicians did not do business with me, but I enjoy sharing my knowledge and helping them to become educated in financial basics. But by giving away this knowledge, when and if they did have a need, or they have acquaintances and friends that had a need, they would come and do business with us. It is a way of establishing a positive relationship with the community.

When my bank started the program at the time, we were lucky enough to be the first in the marketplace. We had a billboard created that read "The Doctors' Banker." This billboard and our education program established and spoke this idea into existence. It fostered many opportunities that allowed our bank to be the first in the market for this kind of program, all through prioritizing and teaching others.

Setting Limits

Of course, when you give, you also have to set some limits, because often takers have no limits. I've found that there are people my friend John Fahey refers to as "time burglars," who will keep asking and taking but never plan to do any business.

My philosophy is that I'll gladly give you the shirt off my back, but don't rip it off. Helping people is in my nature, but protecting your craft is essential. It's all about sharing, not stealing.

Your business is how you live. It's the way you support and raise your family. You can't give away too much, because it's human nature that people will keep on pressing to take more and more if you don't recognize how far you're willing to go and develop limits on what you're willing to do.

For me, the end goal isn't just to get business because people remember how helpful I am. Sometimes, you will give more altruistically because you can. For example, the other day a young woman reached out to me explaining that her job was being eliminated after 15 years. She knew I had a strong network of connections, and she asked if I could pass on her resume. I asked if she had a specific company in mind that she was interested in working for, and she did. I had some contacts there, and so I sent her information on for her.

There is nothing I expect from that intervention expect possibly the good karma that maybe one day someone will help my child if they have a similar situation occur. I have no expectations for that kind of "give away," but I was glad to do it.

On the other hand, if a potential client is constantly calling me for information, there are limits to what I will provide. Occasionally I will make a business proposal to a company, and they will pass, yet that potential client keeps calling, wanting more information or an introduction. At that point, you need to be able to stop sharing, deflect, and provide nothing further, or they may continue to take without ever engaging your business.

I think it is important to remember, particularly if you're a connector, that you've worked to establish those connections. There's no need to give away valuable contacts to someone for a half-hour discussion with them. I have worked more than 25 years to establish my contact list. If someone wants the kind of information that I have worked that long to establish, but they do not want to do business, that is their choice. They can go somewhere else. I will not devalue my work or that of my team and my business. This is essential in the world of consulting.

We see our value in larger terms than in a half-hour paid increment. It's important to protect what you spend time, possibly a lifetime, on building. Giving it away is beneficial to others, and to yourself personally as a good act, an act of sharing. But know your value. Understand what your time and energy is worth. Don't trade a pearl for a piece of gravel.

When we give too much, even when we say we do not expect a return, we can get disappointed. At some point, you may need to raise the guard rails. Remember that if you give too much away, you won't have any left to give to someone else who could truly benefit.

Prevent Burn Out

Setting limits for your giving also prevents burn out and overextending yourself. As an example, Forge was asked to bid on a project for the local city government. To do so, we incurred approximately $3,000 in expenses, and ultimately another provider was chosen, an out of state company. It was disappointing and costly to have that outcome.

When you give too much, even if you don't expect a return, you can get disappointed, as we did when the city contracted with an out-of-state supplier. When someone chooses to do business with someone else after you've helped them and been supportive in the past, burnout and disappointment will follow. It's natural, but another consequence of that disappointment is that you can grow resentful. You can be debilitated in a way that prevents you from acting like the generous person you were created to be.

Protecting yourself from burnout is somewhat of a balancing act. Give as much as you can without giving *yourself* away. Give with integrity. Think about how and why you are giving, and don't cross a line to where your giving takes so much from you that you're no longer able to give back in the areas that are most important to you, or where it will make more of a positive difference in the lives of others.

By setting limits, givers can avoid overextending themselves, which is crucial for maintaining good physical, emotional, and mental health and preventing burnout. Remember to know your own value and maintain it.

Learning to set and enforce limits empowers you to make decisions that are in your best interest rather than feeling compelled to always say yes.

Takeaways

- Have you given away knowledge or information just to help others?
- Can you think of times when giving away information to empower others has provided a positive return on your giving? What about times that it has not?
- Are you able to differentiate between giving of your own volition and being coerced into doing so by the "takers" in this world?
- Can you think of ways to prevent burning out from being giving and generous?

Conclusion

One of my main precepts in life and in business is to do right by others. When you approach the way you do business — as well as your personal life — with tenets of faith, service, and a vision for the future, you'll find that achievement, empowerment, and success will follow.

My experiences with the sport of wrestling, in the military, with my family, and through my faith have all combined to provide me with the discipline and perseverance to move forward in life and in work.

Personally, as both a civic and business leader, I choose to take risks, try new things, and continue to give back to my community and to others through my business. This book is designed to give some of my knowledge in these areas back to you, and to encourage you to share this knowledge.

As a connector, I have been fortunate enough to create a support network that has shaped so many new opportunities and connections for me while also holding me accountable for my own actions. I can't stress enough the importance of establishing connections between people, whether that is members of your own team or perspective clients and customers. I've endeavored here to form a connection with you.

My own strong sense of purpose has led me to believe that in helping others I'm helping myself. I hope that this book helps you to gain a deeper vision and insight into strategic planning and development, both for your business and for your personal life and wellbeing.

Lead With Your Strengths

While there is no single formula for success, leading with your strengths is key. Create and use a blueprint that allows you to follow an orderly and deliberate plan for growth and provides the room to learn from lessons that are bound to occur and continue to grow from them.

One important aspect of your blueprint should always be to establish processes for your business. Creating and detailing the processes that make your business run efficiently today will also serve to make it viable to continue throughout generations or for a sale in the future.

Another aspect of your success is having stakeholders with whom you can interact. Encourage their empowerment, and don't be afraid to step back from micromanaging them. And of course, don't forget to embrace the critic for fresh ideas and alternative viewpoints, but set limits upon them, so that they are not taking advantage of your inclusion or preventing growth.

Be Generous with Your Knowledge

While it is important to share your knowledge with others, don't forget to set limits on those who take from your knowledge and wisdom without giving back. Don't give up on giving. While guarding against burn out, giving back is essential for the good of your community, and the good of your business.

When we share, we help others; and when we help and empower others, we are also empowering ourselves, and our own future, as well as that of our families, our work, and our community. We are establishing connections that last throughout our lives and beyond them.

Is this a tall order? Perhaps, but no more so than allowing yourself to achieve business success.

And along the way, while working with these goals in mind, allow yourself to experience losses and lessons. Failure is nothing to be ashamed of. Embracing adversity as I have had to do, and almost every one of us has done, is the key to rising back up again, to learning, growing, and achieving more than we ever have before.

Remember, you can't appreciate the view from the top of the mountain if you haven't spent time in the valley below.

The key lesson that I have learned on the mat in wrestling, through a lifetime of service both in and out of the military, in my community, and through my faith, is to get back up when you fall. Keep going forward and growing. I hope I have imparted the importance of that to you.

In business, as in all aspects of your life, remember — you can score from the bottom. You can use that pressure, that force, to stand up when you are down and forge ahead.

"The supreme quality for leadership is unquestionably integrity. Without it, no real success is possible, no matter whether it is on a section gang, a football field, in an army, or in an office."

Dwight D. Eisenhower

Acknowledgements

Blessed Beyond Measure...

Like the great Lou Gehrig, I "consider myself the luckiest man on the face of the earth!" My whole life has been supported by wonderful people who have helped me develop as a person, father, husband, leader, coach, and public servant. These are the same people who have opened the doors of opportunity and provided a helping hand when I have failed and fallen short. And trust me, I have done plenty of both.

As a Catholic, I am especially grateful for the foundation of faith that has formed me. My faith does not make me perfect, but it does challenge me to seek righteousness and to be a better person. I am grateful to share my faith with my family and that they too may have hope in the promise that "all things work together for good, to them that love God."

There is no doubt that we are a collection of our experiences. When I think about the opportunities that have come my way, I can't help but to be grateful. To all of our clients, customers, and partners, thank you for your business, the opportunity to serve you, and the trust that you have placed in me and my pursuits over the years. To all the smart people who have worked alongside me, and especially our team at Forge, you made me look good and brought credibility to our work. Thank you to Beth Ryan for lending your editing skills to this book.

As I was growing up, I quickly learned that if I was going to have a chance at success, education would be the great equalizer. I am the beneficiary of a wonderful education provided by caring, thoughtful, and smart teachers. To all my great teachers, professors, coaches, administrators, bus drivers, cafeteria aides, custodians, and everyone that makes up a school family, I am grateful! Especially to Walt L., Ken B., Loraine P., Ron A., Rudy A., and too many others to count, thank you for pouring into me.

To all who have given me mentorship and guidance in business, I am humbled. From my first boss, my grandfather, and so many fine leaders that have taken me under their wing, I appreciate you and the opportunities that you have offered. Throughout landscaping, healthcare, banking, government contracting, military service, and entrepreneurship, my career has been a circuitous route. Glenn A., Mark N., John D., Doug L., John F., Tim S., and Jon H., thank you! Learning from great leaders and people like RADM Virgil Hill, General Alfred Sanelli, Colonel Krine Westhoven, Colonel Billy Murphy, and CSM Harry Harris set an example of excellence for which I am grateful!

While I have made many acquaintances throughout my journey, I have been so fortunate to have a small handful of people in my life that took me in and made me a better person. The Capers family made all the difference by helping me see a better version of myself and striving for the best that life has to offer. Bud, Ruthie, and especially Eric, my best man, and the extended family, you made a difference because I mattered to you. Thank you!

My mom, Pam, always believed in me and showed me what it meant to be a compassionate and caring person. And while my dad, Salvatore, passed away when I was 10 years old, his example and legacy challenges me every day to leave the world a better place than I found it. My grandparents, Charles and Carrie Johnson, made all the difference in my life. They taught me to do good when I can, to be like Christ as much as possible, to be dedicated to family, and to love unconditionally. Your love and encouragement gave me hope. To the Bakos Family, thank you for making me part of your family without reservation or condition. Your love and support are always appreciated.

I am most grateful to be a husband and father. Ashley makes me want to be a better person every day. Her love, intelligence, generosity, work ethic, and serious cooking skills make our family a family. She is the best example for our son Max and daughters Izzy and Cece. Our family is the light of my life, and because of them I consider myself even luckier than Lou Gehrig!

Made in the USA
Columbia, SC
18 October 2024